George W. Cox

A Manual of Mythology

In the Form of Question and Answer

George W. Cox

A Manual of Mythology
In the Form of Question and Answer

ISBN/EAN: 9783337058159

Printed in Europe, USA, Canada, Australia, Japan

Cover: Foto ©ninafisch / pixelio.de

More available books at **www.hansebooks.com**

A MANUAL

OF

MYTHOLOGY

IN THE FORM OF QUESTION AND ANSWER.

BY THE

REV. GEORGE W. COX, M. A.,
LATE SCHOLAR OF TRINITY COLLEGE, OXFORD.

First American, from the Second London Edition.

NEW YORK:
LEYPOLDT & HOLT.
1868.

Entered according to Act of Congress, in the year 1868,

BY LEYPOLDT & HOLT,

In the Clerk's Office of the District Court of the United States for the Southern District of New York.

Stereotyped by LITTLE, RENNIE & CO.,
430 Broome St., New York.

CONTENTS.

	PAGE
Advertisement	7
Preface	9
The Origin and Growth of Mythology	21
GREEK MYTHOLOGY	29
Zeus	29
Poseidon	37
Hades	42
Hêrê, or Hera	45
Hestia	48
Dêmêtêr	51
Athênê, or Athena	58
Ares	63
Aphrodite	67
Hephæstus	72
Phœbus Apollo	75
Artemis	83
Hermes	85
Dionysus	95
Heracles	100
Perseus	110
Theseus	121
Œdipus	125
Procris	135
Orpheus	138
Europa	141
Meleagros (Meleager)	144

GREEK MYTHOLOGY—

	PAGE
Phaethon	148
Asklepios (Æsculapius)	151
Admetus	154
Lycaon	155
Deucalion	158
Io	162
Epimetheus	166
Dædalus	169
Niobe	171
Tantalus	172
Ixion	175
Bellerophon, or Bellerophontes	178
Skylla (Scylla)	181
Iamos	183
Amphiaraos	185
Briareos (Briareus)	187
Arethusa	188
Tyro	189
Narcissus	190
The Argonauts	191
The Tale of Troy	198
The return of the Heroes from Troy	216
Inhabitants of the Greek Mythical World	228

LATIN MYTHOLOGY 237

Jupiter	238
Neptune	239
Pluto	240
Vesta	240
Ceres	241
Minerva	241
Mars	242
Venus	243

CONTENTS.

LATIN MYTHOLOGY— PAGE
   Vulcan... 244
   Apollo... 244
   Diana and Janus............................. 244
   Mercury... 245
   Æsculapius..................................... 245
   Bacchus... 246
   Hercules.. 246
   Saturn... 249
   Aurora... 250
   Avernus... 250
   Latin deities not identified with Greek gods...... 251
EGYPTIAN MYTHOLOGY............................ 257
ASSYRIAN MYTHOLOGY............................ 260
THE MYTHOLOGY OF THE VEDA.................. 263
PERSIAN MYTHOLOGY............................. 270
NORSE MYTHOLOGY................................. 273

APPENDIX.

Mythical Genealogies................................. 283
Index... 291

ADVERTISEMENT.

THE researches of Comparative Mythologists during the present century have effected a complete revolution in the treatment and classification of the various systems of mythology.

The present Manual, which is an attempt to give the results of those researches in a form suitable for the young, must necessarily differ widely from the manuals or elementary works which have preceded it. But no apology seems to be needed for changes which remove from our common heritage of mythical tradition all that may appear gross and repulsive in it, and exhibit the exquisite poetry which lies at the root of all these ancient stories.

In some portions of the subject, differences of opinion must still exist. I have, therefore, been careful to make no statements of any importance for which I cannot claim the authority of such writers as Niebuhr, Thirlwall, Grimm, Max Müller, Kuhn, Muir, Cornewall Lewis, Grote, Dasent, and Bréal. The Comparative Mythologist must still say with Grimm: "I shall indeed interpret all that I can, but I cannot interpret all that I should like." I venture, therefore, to add, that for any suggestions or remarks which may be forwarded to me through the publishers, I shall feel grateful. My obligations to Professor Max Müller I thankfully acknowledge.

The sections on Vedic, Persian, and Teutonic Mythology are short; but a lengthened treatment of these systems would have swelled the volume to too great a size; and many names which are not specially mentioned in those sections, have been noticed with sufficient fulness in the section on Greek Mythology.

The references given in the text of the answers, are to the tales in which the myth or legend under notice has been recounted at length.[1]

The quantity of syllables in the several names, is, in all cases which may appear doubtful, given in the Index.

---

[1] Cox's Tales of Ancient Greece, soon to be published by Leypoldt & Holt.

PREFACE.

I HOPE that students who may have to use this little book will read the few sentences which I write by way of preface.

You may have heard the stories which are told about Apollo, or Prometheus, or Tantalus; and you may have thought them uninteresting, or tiresome, or horrible. The deeds which they are said to have done may have seemed to you (as they seemed to many good men among the old Greeks and Romans) the deeds of savages; and you may have asked, "Why should we learn these things at all, and what good will it do us to know them?"

You may, perhaps, have been also puzzled by the many names which you were obliged to learn without attaching any meaning to them, and by the ranks or classes into which the gods and heroes were divided; and thus you may have seen nothing good or beautiful in your task to make up for what was dull or disagreeable in it.

And yet these old stories about Greek gods, and nymphs, and Titans, are amongst the loveliest things which men have ever imagined, as you will see, I think, if you follow me in what I am now going to say.

Many ages ago, long before Europe had any of the nations who now live in it, and while everything was new and strange to the people who then lived on the earth, men talked of the things which they saw and heard, in a way very different from our way of speaking now. We talk of the sun rising and setting, as of something which is sure to happen : but they did not know enough to feel sure about these things ; and so when the evening came, they said, "Our friend the sun is dead; will he come back again?" and when they saw him once more in the east, they rejoiced because he brought back their light and their life with him. Knowing very little about themselves, and nothing at all of the things which they saw in the world around them, they fancied that everything had the same kind of life which they had themselves. In this way they came to think that the sun and stars, the rivers and streams, could see, and feel, and think, and that they shone or moved of their own accord. Thus they spoke of everything as if it were alive, and instead of saying, as we say, that the morning comes before the sunrise, and that the evening twilight follows the sunset, they spoke of the sun as the lover of the dawn or morning who went before him, as longing to overtake her, and as killing her with his bright rays, which shone like spears. We talk of the clouds which scud along the sky; but they spoke of the cows of the sun, which the children of the morning drove every day to their pastures in the blue fields of heaven. So, too, when the sun set, they said that the dawn, with its soft and tender light, had come to soothe her son or her husband in his dying hour. In the same way, the sun was the child of darkness, and in the morning he wove for his bride in the heavens a fairy network of clouds, which reappeared when she came back to him in the evening. When the sun shone with a pleasant warmth, they spoke of him as the friend of men: when his scorching heat brought a drought, they said that the sun was slaying his children, or that some one else, who knew not how to guide them, was driving the horses of his chariot through the sky. As they looked on the dark clouds which rested on the earth without giving any rain, they said that the terrible being whom they named the snake or dragon was shutting up the waters in a prison-house. When the thunder rolled, they said that this hateful monster was uttering his hard riddles; and when, at last, the rain burst forth, they said that the bright sun had slain his enemy, and brought a stream of life for the thirsting earth.

Now, so long as men remained in the same place, there was no fear that the words which they spoke would be misunderstood: but as time went on they were scattered, and some wandered to the south, and some to the north and west; and so it came to pass that they kept the names which they gave to the sun and the clouds and all other things, when their meaning had been almost or quite forgotten. In this way they still spoke of Phœbus as loving Daphne, after they had forgotten that this meant only "The Sun loves the Dawn." So the name of the dew had been Procris, and it had been said that the sun killed (dried up) the dew as he rose in the sky: but now Kephalos (Cephalus) became a man who, without knowing it, killed a woman named Procris, whom he loved. Instead of saying any more that the moon came to see the sun die, they said that Selênê came to look on Endymion, or that Antigone soothed Œdipus in his last hour. Instead of saying that the sun was the child of darkness, they said that Phœbus was the son of Leto; and in place of the fairy network of clouds, they spoke of the robe which Helios gave to the wise maiden Medea. So, too, the dragon or snake which imprisoned the rain in the clouds, became the Sphinx, and the sun, who smote it, was turned into Œdipus, who alone could understand her dark sayings and deliver men from the plague of drought.

But some of these tales, when so changed, became coarse or horrible, or even disgusting. Long ago men had said that the sun, when he glared too fiercely, killed the fruits which his warmth was ripening, or that he dried up the streams over which he passed; but when they had forgotten the meaning of the old names, they spoke of the king Tantalus, who killed and roasted his own child, and set him on the banquet-table of the gods. It was the same with the stories told of Heracles (Hercules), which had once been only a name of the sun. We, too, might speak now of the sun as "coming forth like a bridegroom out of his chamber," as " rejoicing as a giant to run his course," and as " going about from one end of heaven to the other;"[1] we might say that wherever he goes the earth smiles under his pleasant light, and yields her fruit with gladness. But when, instead of thinking of the sun, they fancied that Heracles was a man, then the story went that, although he was strong, and brave, and kind, yet he never remained with those whom he had loved, but constantly found new brides in many lands; and just as we might speak of the sun as feasting on the fruits of the earth, so Heracles became a man very fond of eating and drinking, and at last was changed into something like a clown or a buffoon.

Thus, then, mythology, as we call it now, is simply a collection of the sayings by which men once upon a time described whatever they saw and heard in the countries where they lived. This key, which has unlocked almost all the secrets of mythology, was placed in our hands by Professor Max Müller, who has done more than all other writers to bring out the exquisite and touching poetry that underlies these ancient legends. He has shown us that in this

[1] Psalm xix. 5, 6.

their first shape, these sayings were all perfectly natural, and marvellously beautiful and true. We see the lovely evening twilight die out before the coming night; but when they saw this, they said that the beautiful Eurydike (Eurydice) had been stung by the serpent of darkness, and that Orpheus was gone to fetch her back from the land of the dead. We see the light which had vanished in the west reappear in the east; but they said that Eurydike was now returning to the earth. And as this tender light is seen no more when the sun himself is risen, they said that Orpheus had turned round too soon to look at her, and so was parted from the wife whom he loved so dearly.

And as it is with this sad and beautiful tale, so it is with all those which may seem to you coarse or dull or ugly. They are so only because the real meaning of the names has been half forgotten or wholly lost. Œdipus and Perseus, we are told, killed their parents, but it is only because the sun was said to kill the darkness from which it seems to spring. So again, it was said that the sun was united in the evening to the light from which he rose in the morning: but in the later story it was said that Œdipus became the husband of his mother

Iocastê (Jocasta), and a terrible history was built up on this notion.

But, as you see, none of these fearful or disgusting stories were ever made on purpose. No one ever sat down to describe gods and great heroes as doing things which all decent men would be ashamed to think of. There can scarcely be a greater mistake than to suppose that whole nations were suddenly seized with a strange madness, which drove them to invent all sorts of ridiculous and contemptible tales, and that every nation has at some time or other gone mad in this way. You must not fancy that things so foolish and wicked were done, especially by that people who have left us the beautiful legends of Demeter, and Niobe, and Cadmus, of Helen and Œnone, of Perseus and Sarpedon. It may be very absurd to be told that Cronos (the father of Zeus, or Jupiter) swallowed his own children; but we know it is not absurd to say that time swallows up the days which spring from it; and the old phrase meant simply this and nothing more, although before the people came to Greece they had forgotten its meaning.

Thus we may look upon mythology as on something exceedingly beautiful, over which much dust has settled, disfiguring some parts and hiding others. Most of this dust we are able now to sweep away, and then the jewels hidden beneath it shine again in all their brilliance and purity. You may be sure that in all these tales there is nothing of which, in its old shape, we ought to be ashamed, and that, when you have lifted the veil which conceals them, you will find only true and beautiful thoughts which are as much ours as ever they were the thoughts of men who lived in that very early time.

The task of removing this covering is generally as easy as it is delightful. <u>Many of these</u> tales, perhaps most of them, explain themselves. <u>Phœbus (the shining one</u>) is born in <u>Delos (the bright land</u>); he is the son of <u>Leto (the darkness</u>); he slays the children of <u>Niobe (the clouds which are dried up by the sun</u>). Europa (the <u>broad shining morning</u>) is the daughter of Telephassa (who gleams from afar). The cattle of <u>Helios (the sun</u>) are driven to their pastures by Phaethusa and Lampetiê, the *bright* and *glistening* children of Neaira (the early morning). So, as the <u>sun goes from east to west</u>, Europa is carried westward, and Telephassa dies on the western plains of Thessaly, just as the twilight dies out in the western sky.

I need say no more to show that these old stories contain the truest and the most touching poetry—poetry which may make us cheerful or sad, gay or grave, happy or mournful, just as we might feel if from a mountain-top we were to watch the shortlived glories of morning and evening tide. Nor is any thing more needed to show you that in the mythology, whether of Greece or Germany or Norway, there is nothing which should make you less upright and simple, while there is much in it which you may be the better and the happier for knowing. All its disagreeable features are simply distortions, caused by forgetting the original meaning of words; and when these are removed, we shall see only things true and beautiful, lovely and of good report: we shall find there only the simple thoughts of childlike men on the wonderful works of God, and nothing which we can laugh at, or despise, or pity. Their words will make us feel as we feel when we look on the glory and beauty of the heavens and the earth, that the thoughts of God are very deep, and that we have the same joys and sufferings, the same fears and hopes, which were felt by these men and women of old time. And as you read some of these tales, you will begin to understand how

God led them on, slowly perhaps, yet surely, to the consciousness that He was a loving and righteous Father, and that it is He who made the sun and moon and all other things in their season. You will see that the Greek or the Roman did not pray to the Zeus or the Jupiter who was unjust, or coarse, or tyrannical. The god to whom they prayed in times of need or sorrow was indeed *named* Zeus (or Jupiter), but he was, as their own poets expressed it, the great and holy God who made all things, and in whom all things live and move and have their being.

When you come to see this, you may be thankful that you learnt something about this old mythology, which grew up slowly without any wilfully evil thoughts in the minds of Greeks or Romans or any other people. The process was simple, and it could not be avoided. They never sat down to arrange their gods and heroes in ranks or classes. The order in which they are sometimes given is the work of a very late age; and if we fix our minds upon it, it will hinder rather than help us in our efforts to understand these legends.

I hope that what I have now said may be clear and intelligible to all. But if any thing should still seem dark, it will probably not long remain so. The key now placed in your hands will unlock almost every door, and wherever you go, you will find something which will amply repay you for your trouble. It is scarcely too much to say that in these old legends we have " a fountain of delight which no man can ever drain dry ;" and this delight will, I trust, be felt by all whom this little book is meant to teach.

THE ORIGIN AND GROWTH OF MYTHOLOGY.

1. What is mythology?

A collection of tales or legends relating to the gods, heroes, demons, or other beings whose names have been preserved in popular belief.

2. Are such tales found only in the traditions of the ancient Greeks and Romans?

No; every nation has had its mythology, and

some nations still retain their old faith in these stories. Thus we have the mythology not only of Greece and Rome, but of India, Persia, Norway, Germany, and other countries.

3. What circumstance is especially forced on our notice when we compare the legends of these different lands?

The close resemblance which runs through them in all their most important features.

4. What is the conclusion to be drawn from this?

That the legends of all these nations have one common source.

5. And what is this source?

The words or phrases used by the most ancient tribes in speaking of the things which they saw, heard, or felt in the world around them.

6. If these words related to things of every-day life, how came they to give rise to stories about giants and nymphs and other unreal beings?

Because, as time went on, and the people were scattered, the meaning of the old words was either wholly or in part forgotten.

7. How is this proved?

By the fact that many names, which in Greek and Latin have no meaning, are perfectly intelligible in other languages.

8. Give some instances.

Such names as Argynnis, Phoroneus, and Erinys, are, in Greek, words which convey no sense: in the old mythology of India they explain themselves. Erinys is thus seen to be the dawn as it *creeps* along the sky; Argynnis is a name for the morning, denoting its brilliance; and Phoroneus is the god of fire, Bhuranyu.

9. Mention an instance in which the old meaning of the words was not wholly forgotten.

In the story of Endymion, Selene, who visits him, is still the moon; all that had been forgotten was that Endymion is a name for the sun as he plunges into the sea: and thus it was thought that Endymion was some young man on whom the moon looked down lovingly.

10. Do many names in Greek mythology explain themselves in this way?

Yes. Perhaps the greater number do so. Thus Phœbus means lord of *light* or of *life;* and Delos, where he is born, means the *bright* land. Hence he is also called Lykegenes, *sprung from light.* His mother is Leto (Latona), which means the night, from which the sun seems to spring. So too Endymion, the setting sun, sleeps in Latmos, the land of forgetfulness.

11. In these tales are the same names, or names very like each other, given both to men and women?

Yes. The mother of Cadmus and Europa is Telephassa, which means "she who shines from far." This is only another form of the name Telephus, who is also a child of Augê, *the light.* So too the names Europa and Eurytus, Eurymedon, Euryanassa, Euryphassa, with many others, all denote *a broad spreading* light, like that of the dawn as it rushes across the sky.

12. Do the incidents in these tales resemble each other as closely as the names?

Yes. In a very large number of legends the parents, warned that their son will destroy them, expose their children, who are saved by some wild beast and brought up by some herdsman. The children so recovered always grow up beautiful, brave, strong, and generous; but, either unconsciously or against their will, they fulfil the warnings given before their birth, and become the destroyers of their parents.

13. Mention any tales which thus resemble each other.

Perseus, Œdipus, Cyrus, Romulus, Paris, are all exposed as infants, are all saved from death, and discovered by the splendor of their countenances and the dignity of their bearing. Either consciously or unconsciously, Perseus kills Acrisios, Œdipus kills Laios, Cyrus slays Astyages, Romulus kills Amulius, and Paris brings about the ruin of Priam and the city of Troy.

14. Have these stories any other features in common?

Yes. These heroes have generally a short but brilliant life, and have to labor for others, not for themselves. Thus Heracles (Hercules) is a slave to Eurystheus, Achilles goes to Troy for no quarrel of his own, and Perseus has to toil at the bidding of king Polydectes. They are all of them slayers of monsters, and in other ways helpers of men. Thus Bellerophon kills Belleros and Chimæra, Perseus destroys the Gorgon Medusa, Theseus kills the Minotaur, Œdipus slays the Sphinx, and Phœbus Apollo kills the serpent Python.

15. Are these things repeated in the stories of other countries?

Yes. In the Indian tales Indra kills the dragon Vritra, and in the Old Norse legend Sigurd kills the great snake Fafnir. In the Persian story, Rustem is as brave and mighty as Heracles, and his exploits are of the same kind. All of them have invincible spears or swords, and can be wounded only in one spot, or by one kind of weapon only.

16. Do these heroes resemble each other in person and character, as well as in the general course of their lives?

Yes. They all have fair faces, and golden locks flowing over their shoulders. They all sacrifice their own ease for the good of others, and yet are all tempted to forsake or leave the brides of their youth. Thus Heracles goes away from Iolê, Paris forsakes Œnone, Theseus leaves Ariadne, and Sigurd deserts Brynhild. They are also subject to strange fits of gloom and sullenness, and every thing grows dark in their absence from the banquet or the battle-field. But in the end they come forth in all their early glory, and are forgiven by the women whom they had wronged.

17. What do we learn from these resemblances?

That they cannot be accidental; and as we know that Greeks, and Romans, and Hindus, and Germans, and Norsemen, could not have copied these tales from one another three or four thousand years ago, we must trace them to a common source, when the forefathers of all these tribes were living in the same place.

18. What, then, is the root or germ of all these stories?

Words, or phrases, which described events or scenes in the outward world. Thus, whereas in the oldest Hindu hymns the Sun is said to love the Dawn, and as the Sun kills the Dew when he looks on it, the Greeks said that Phœbus loved Daphne, and that Procris was killed by Kephalos (Cephalus).

19. But how do we know that the stories are really the same?

Because words like Procris, Daphne, Briseis, Hermes, Charites, and Echidna, which have no clear meaning in Greek, are, in the ancient language of India, merely common names for the Dew and the Sun, for the morning with its beautiful clouds and soft breezes, for the glistening horses of the Sun and the throttling snake of darkness.

20. What was the consequence of this forgetfulness of the first meaning of words?

That many of the tales became unnatural and even shocking. Thus, whereas, in time of drought, men had said that the Sun was killing the fruits of the Earth which was his bride, the Greek said that Tantalus, an Eastern king, killed and cooked his own child. So, too, it had once been said that, after slaying noxious things and cheering the earth with his brightness, the Sun was united in the evening with the Dawn whom he had forsaken in the morning. But when the Greeks had forgotten what was meant by the name of Œdipus, they said that, after slaying the Sphinx, he was married to his own mother, and that terrible evils and sufferings followed this event.

21. How, then, are we to look on such stories?

We should look on them as on perfectly harmless and beautiful tales, which have been gradually disfigured, without the will or even the consciousness of those who so changed them.

22. What light do they throw on the earliest history of the European nations?

They show that the ancestors of Englishmen and Germans, of Norwegians, and Italians, and Greeks, all had the same thoughts, hopes, and fears which we feel now, and that, on the whole, these thoughts were very beautiful and true.

23. What, then, were these phrases which gave rise to so many tales?

They form the language of all true poets in all times and countries. Everywhere they attribute life to the things which they see and hear around them; the Sun is for them a bridegroom coming out of his chamber, and a giant rejoicing to run his course. This idea is the groundwork of the legends of Heracles, Perseus, Theseus, Achilles, Bellerophon, and very many others; and all whose hearts and minds are open to see the works of God, will feel both their truth and their beauty.

GREEK MYTHOLOGY.

ZEUS.

24. Who was the supreme god in the mythology of the Greeks?

Zeus, who, before the time when the Iliad and Odyssey were composed, had come to be regarded as the father of all gods and men.

25. Had he not then always been the highest god?

No. According to some stories, there was a time when Cronos, his father, was supreme; but even Cronos was not first in the order of the gods.

26. Were the gods, then, arranged in some fixed order?

Not at first; but in later times the poets compared the different tales that were told about the various gods, and then arranged them according to the relationship pointed out in each story.

27. Did these stories differ much from one another?

So much that it is often impossible to make them agree together, and we can only say, in many cases, that each country or city followed its own version.

28. Is this the case with the legends of Zeus and the gods who went before him?

Yes. In one account, the first beings are Chaos and Gaia, from whom spring Ouranos (or Uranus) and the Great Mountains and Pontus. In another, Gaia or Gê (the Earth) is the wife of Ouranos; and their children, Hyperion, Iapetus, and many others, are born before Cronos, the father of Zeus.

29. Who is Ouranos?

Ouranos is the heaven which is spread like a veil over the earth, and is the same as the old Hindu god Varuna, whose name comes from a root, *var*, meaning to veil or conceal.

30. What is the legend of Cronos?

It is said that Ouranos hurled the Cyclopes,

with Bronte, Sterope (Thunder and Lightning), and other children of Gaia (the Earth), into the abyss called Tartarus; and that Gaia, in her grief and anger, urged her other children to mutilate their father and to set up Cronos instead upon his throne.

31. What were the acts of Cronos as soon as he became king?

He is said to have swallowed his children soon after each was born.

32. How is this to be explained?

As the action of time, which swallows up the days as they come each in its order.

33. What had these acts of Cronos to do with the history of Zeus?

Rhea, the wife of Cronos and the mother of Zeus, anxious to save her child, gave her husband a stone to swallow, while Zeus was born and nourished in the cave of Dicte or on Ida.

34. Is the name *Zeus* found in the Hindu mythology?

Yes. Zeus is there Dyaus, the god of the bright sky or heaven, from a word which means *to shine*.

35. Is it found also in the tales of other nations?

Yes. As the Hindus spoke of Dyaus-pitar, and the Greeks of Zeus Patêr, so the Latins and Romans called him Jupiter, which means *father Zeus*. By the Anglo-Saxons he was called Tiu (a word which is still seen in our *Tuesday*), and by the old High Germans he was known as Zio.

36. What, then, was the first meaning of the name?

It meant the pure blue sky, the abode of light, far above the clouds or any thing which could sully its purity.

37. Does this at all explain the Greek story?

It shows us why Zeus is born in the cave of Dicte, which is another of those words that denote the approach of light, just as Delos, where Phœbus is born, is the *bright land*.

38. What acts are ascribed to Zeus after he had come to his full strength?

He is said to have delivered the Cyclopes from Tartarus, and to have obtained the aid of the hundred-handed giants in his war against the Titans.

39. Was he aided by any others in this struggle?

According to the story followed by Æschylus, he had the help of Prometheus, the son of Deucalion, and by his aid he dethroned Cronos; but angry afterward, because Prometheus taught men the use of fire, he chained him to the rugged rocks of Caucasus.

40. How was the empire of Cronos divided?

We are told in some stories that the Cyclopes gave to Zeus a thunderbolt, and to his brothers Hades and Poseidon a helmet and a trident, and that, having received these gifts, the three gods cast lots, and the sovereignty of heaven fell to the portion of Zeus, that of the sea to Poseidon, and that of the lower regions to Hades.

41. What is the character of Zeus in the Homeric poems?

Zeus in these poems is described in ways so different that we should rather say that there were two gods called by this name. Sometimes he is represented as partial, unjust, fond of rest and pleasure, changeable in his affections, and unfaithful in his love, greedy, sensual, and impure. But in hours of real trouble and grief, Achilles and the other Achaians pray to a Zeus who is not only irresistible in might, but also just and righteous.

42. How is this contrast to be accounted for?

As the Indian word Dyaus seems originally to have been a name for the One only God, so it was retained by the Greeks and other kindred peoples to express all that they felt toward God. But as the word also meant the visible sky, with its clouds and vapors, some of the phrases which described its changes came, when their meaning was forgotten, to denote vile or shameful actions. Thus the earth had been spoken of as the bride of the sky, and the sky was said to overshadow the earth with his love in every land; and all this, when applied to a deity with human form and passions, grew up into strange stories of lawless license.

43. Is this conclusion justified by the later Greek poetry?

It is even strengthened, for while in Hesiod the descent of the gods, their earthly loves, and their gross actions are brought out even more prominently, yet the poet can turn sharply away from all such things to the thought of that pure and holy Zeus who looks down from heaven to see if men will do justice and seek after God.

44. How was this contrast felt by the poets and philosophers of a still later age?

By some, the thought that the gods must be good was regarded as a sufficient reason for disbelieving all stories to their discredit: by others these tales were considered to disprove their divinity, as Euripides said—

"If the gods do aught unseemly, then they are not gods at all."

But others rested content with the knowledge that Zeus was a mere name by which they might speak of Him in whom we live, and move, and have our being; but which is utterly unable to express, as our mind is to conceive, His infinite perfection.

45. Has the name Zeus passed into any other form?

It is derived from the same root with the Greek Theos and the Latin Deus, which both mean "God." The former word forms part of the word "Theology," which means what we think or believe about God.

46. Who are named as the children of Zeus?

Apollo and Artemis, whose mother was called Leto (Latona), Ares, Hermes, and Athena, who, with Poseidon, Hera, Hephæstus, Hestia, Demeter, Aphrodite, and Zeus himself, formed the body which in the days of Thucydides was worshipped as "the twelve gods" of Olympus.

47. Is this ordering of the gods found in the Homeric poems?

No. Many of the deities in these poems are not nearly so important as they are in later times, while many become lower in character in later tradition.

48. What is the name given to those poems which describe the birth and attributes of the gods?

They are called theogonies; the best known being the theogony of Hesiod, and that which bears the name of Orpheus.

49. Which were the most celebrated temples or sanctuaries of Zeus in ancient Hellas or Greece?

The temple on Mount Lycæus (a word denoting merely *brightness*), in Arcadia; that of Dodona, which at first was in Thessaly, and afterward in Epirus; and that of Olympia in Elis, where the great Olympic games were celebrated at the end of every fourth year.

50. Was Zeus worshipped under many names?

Yes. The number of these names is so great that it would be useless to reckon them. He was named sometimes from places, as the Dodonæan, Pelasgic, or Cretan Zeus, but more commonly he was invoked as the fountain of order, justice, law, and equity. Thus he was called Ephestios, as guarding family life, Horkios, as watching over contracts, and Xenios, as the protector of strangers.

51. What do these many names teach us?

That they express only some one or more of those good qualities which were felt to make up the nature, not of Zeus, the son of Cronos, but of the One Great God and Father of us all.

POSEIDON.

52. Who was Poseidon?

A son of Cronos and Rhea, and therefore a brother of Zeus and Hades.

53. What was his office?

When the lots were cast for the sovereignty of the heavens, the sea, and the regions beneath the earth, that of the sea fell to the share of Poseidon, who received a trident as the emblem of his power.

54. In what sense is Poseidon the god of the sea?

Seemingly as having under his control the

forces which affect its movements, rather than as himself inhabiting its waters.

55. Is there, then, any god whose actual home is in the sea?

Yes; Nereus lives in the deep waters, and stands to Poseidon in the same relation which Helios, who dwells in the sun, bears to Phœbus, the lord of light.

56. What is the meaning of the name Poseidon?

It is not known with certainty.

57. Is there any thing in the legends which may throw light on the meaning of the name?

In the Iliad and Odyssey Poseidon is represented as equal to Zeus in dignity, and inferior to him only in might. He has also the power of creation, for, according to one story, he is the maker of the horse. He is also called Gaiêochos, the keeper of the earth, and Enosichthon, the world-shaker; and lastly, he disputes with Hera, Helios, and Athena the sovereignty of certain Greek cities. Hence it is not unlikely that the name denoted originally simply the idea of lordship or power, and that it is connected with such words as *potent* and *despot;* Hera, the wife of Zeus, being also called Potnia, or the mighty one.

58. How is Poseidon described as behaving toward Zeus?

He is represented generally as faithful and submissive to the great ruler of Olympus; but once he plotted, we are told, with Hera and Pallas Athena to put Zeus in chains, and was outwitted by Thetis, at whose warning Zeus placed the hundred-handed Briareos by his throne, to scare the conspirators.

59. Where was the palace of Poseidon?

In the deep waters near Ægæ, on the shores of Euboea. Here he kept his horses with golden manes, which answer to the Hindu Harits, or glistening horse of the sun, and which bear him with mighty strides over the sea.

60. Do the legends of Poseidon differ in any special way from those of Zeus?

Yes. Zeus is never described as subject to the will of others, or as compelled to go through servile tasks. But Poseidon is made, together with Heracles, to build the walls of Troy for Laomedon, just as Phœbus Apollo is compelled to be a servant in the house of Admetus.

61. What was the recompense of Poseidon for this service?

The usual recompense of those gods and heroes who, like the sun, are said to toil for the benefit of man. Laomedon refused to pay the promised price, just as Achilles complains that he has all the hardships and none of the rewards of war.

62. What was the consequence of this treachery?

That Poseidon took the side of Agamemnon and Menelaus, when they came to Troy to take vengeance for the evil deeds of Paris.

63. Where is Poseidon said to have created the horse?

At Athens, where there was a contest between him and Athena for the naming of the city. Zeus decided that it should be named after the deity who should confer the best gift on mankind. Upon this Athena produced the olive-tree, and Poseidon the horse; and the victory was adjudged to Athena, the olive being a sign of peace and prosperity, and the horse a sign of war and wretchedness.

64. Is there any other version of this legend?

In the Iliad Achilles tells quite another tale, for he says that Poseidon created the horse in Thessaly, and that he gave the immortal steeds Xanthos and Balios (the *golden* and *spotted*) to Peleus, the father of Achilles.

65. Are any other contests ascribed to Poseidon like that which he had with Athena?

He is said to have claimed authority over

Corinth against Helios (the Sun), over Naxos against Dionysus, and over Ægina against Zeus himself.

66. What do such statements seem to prove?

That originally Poseidon was regarded simply as ruler or king, and that his power was, in process of time, limited to the control of the sea.

67. Who is mentioned as the wife of Poseidon?

Amphitrite.

68. What is the meaning of this name?

It cannot be explained by any word in the Greek language; but in the old Hindu legends we find a god, Trita, who reigns over the water and the air. This name Trita, which some have connected with that of Amphitrite, reappears apparently in Tritopator, a name for the winds, and in Tritogeneia, an epithet applied to Athena, as well as in Triton, the son of Poseidon.

69. Is this name found in the legends of any other people besides the Greeks and Hindus?

Yes. In the old Persian stories, the Trita or Traitana of India reappears as Thraetana, the slayer of the serpent Zohak, which answers to the dragon Python killed by Phœbus, and to Fafnir, who is slain by Sigurd.

HADES.

70. Who was Hades?

Like Poseidon, he was a son of Cronos and Rhea, and brother of Zeus.

71. Over what region was Hades king?

Over the unseen abodes beneath the earth,—the earth, according to the old belief, being regarded as a flat surface.

72. He is, then, the god of the unseen world. Does the name bear out this idea?

It seems to do so, for we have other forms of the word, as Aïdes and Aïdoneus, which appear to denote that which is *unseen,* and the helmet given to him by the Cyclopes had the power of rendering the wearer invisible.

73. How do we know this?

Because Perseus, who is suffered to wear this helmet, becomes invisible so long as he has it on his head, and is again visible when he takes it in his hand. It is, in short, the invisible cap of the Nibelungen tale.

74. Who was the wife of Hades?

Persephonê, or Persephassa, the daughter of Demeter.

75. How did he win her to be his bride?

He is said to have seized her while she was gathering flowers in the fields of Enna, and to have carried her away to his dark abode in a chariot drawn by four coal-black horses.

76. Was Hades known by any other names?

Yes. He was called Plouton, or Pluto, as being guardian of all those mineral treasures of the earth which Andvari, the dwarf, guards in the Teutonic story of Sigurd. He was also known as Polydegmon (the king who *receives many* into his unseen home), a name only slightly varied in Polydectes, the king of Seriphos, who persecutes Danaê, the mother of Perseus.

77. Was he ever described in any other way?

Sometimes he was spoken of as the Zeus of the lower world, and thus the three names, Zeus, Hades, and Poseidon seem to have denoted merely the ideas of sovereignty and power, before they came to be assigned to the local rulers of the sky, the sea, and the nether world.

78. How was the palace of Hades guarded?

By the monstrous dogs Orthros and Kerberos (Cerberus), the latter of whom has three heads.

79. Are these monsters mentioned in the traditions of any other people?

Yes. They reappear as Vritra and Sarvara, names applied to the powers of darkness in the ancient traditions of the Hindus.

80. How was it that Hades, being, like Zeus, a son of Cronos, was not reckoned among the twelve gods of Olympus?

Merely because his empire lay beneath the earth. In the Homeric poems this distinction is not known. There he has the power of going to Olympus when he pleases, and he does so when he is wounded by Heracles.

81. What was the later meaning of the name Hades?

It came to denote not merely the king of the unseen world beneath the earth, but the unseen world itself.

HERE, OR HERA.

82. Who was Hera?

A daughter of Cronos and Rhea, and therefore a sister of Zeus, Hades, and Poseidon. She was also the wife of Zeus.

83. What is the meaning of the name?

It is probably derived from the same root from which come the Sanskrit *svar*, the bright sky, and *sûrya*, the sun, as well as the Greek *Hêlios*, the sun. It seems originally to have meant the heavenly air, the consort of Zeus, the heavenly light.

84. Do the mythical tales support this explanation?

Yes: the story of Ixion especially agrees closely with this its original meaning.

85. How is she described in the Homeric poems?

As the wife of Zeus, who is reverenced by the gods not less than her husband, to whom she is on the whole submissive.

86. What exceptions are there to this submissiveness?

Apart from her opposition to Zeus in the Trojan war, she shared in the plot of Poseidon and Athena to put him in chains.

87. What accounts are given of her birthplace and her marriage?

The stories vary so much that it is impossible to arrange them, or to harmonize them.

88. Who were the children of Hera?

Ares, Hebe, and Hephæstus.

89. What made her take part against the Trojans in the war waged by the Achaians against Troy or Ilion?

The judgment of Paris, before whom Hera, Aphrodite, and Athena appeared as claimants of the golden apple, which was to be given to the fairest of the three. The apple was given to Aphrodite, and from that time forth Hera and Athena are said to have hated the city of Priam.

90. What is the name of the wife of Jupiter in the mythology of the Latins?

Juno.

91. Are Juno and Hera the same deity?

Yes. Although commonly the Latin deities correspond in name only with those of the Greek, in this case the identity is sufficiently proved.

92. How?

As the Hindu *dyavan* represents the Greek Zeus, so the latter answers to the Latin Dianus, or Janus, while the feminine forms, Diana and Juno, would correspond to a Greek Zenon, as a feminine.

93. Do any of the stories told about her explain the nature of her office?

In the greater number she appears as the queen of the pure heaven. This idea is specially manifested in the legend of Ixion (the whirling sun), who, after being purified by Zeus from the guilt of blood, seeks to win the love of Hera, and is cheated by Zeus with a cloud which is made to assume her shape.[1]

---

[1] Tales of Ancient Greece. Ixion.

HESTIA.

94. Who was Hestia?

The eldest child of Cronos and Rhea.

95. What was her office?

She was the goddess of the household hearth, or rather of the fire burning on the hearth. As, according to the old heathen custom, all men were regarded as enemies unless by a special compact they had been made friends, so Hestia presided especially over true and faithful dealing; and as the household was the centre of all kindly affections, she was represented always as pure and undefiled.

96. What is the history of this goddess?

Little more is told of Hestia than that Poseidon sought to have her as his wife and that she refused.

97. How is it that so little is said about her?

Because her name was one of those words which had not lost its meaning. Hestia continued to the end, as she had been from the beginning, the household altar, the sanctuary of peace and equity, and the source of all happiness and wealth.

98. Was Hestia, then, an unimportant deity?

No. The influence of Hestia was perhaps more deeply felt, and wrought more good, than that of any other Olympian deity. Her worship involved direct and practical duties. She could not be fitly served by men who broke their plighted word, or dealt treacherously with those whom they had received at their hearth; and thus her worship was almost an unmixed good both for households and for the State.

99. Was Hestia, then, worshipped by cities as well as in private homes?

Yes. Each town had its Prytaneium, where the prytanes or elders held their meetings. There the sacred fire, burning on the public hearth, was never suffered to die out. If at any time it went out, either from neglect or by accident, it was restored by fire obtained by rubbing pieces of wood together, or by kindling them with a burning-glass, and never by ordinary fire.

100. When a city sent out men to form a colony, how was the bond of union with the parent State kept up?

By the sacred fire of Hestia, a portion of which was carried away by the colonists, to be kept alive forever in their new home; and as long as this fire continued burning, they felt they still had a common interest with the citizens of their old country.

101. Was the office of Hestia limited to the hearths of households and cities?

No. It was supposed that in the centre of the earth there was a hearth which answered to the hearth placed in the centre of the whole universe.

102. Was Hestia worshipped by other nations besides the Greeks?

Yes. By the Latins and Romans, under the name of Vesta, which is only another form of the same word.

DEMETER.

103. Who was Dêmêtêr?

A daughter of Cronos and Rhea, and a sister of Zeus, Poseidon, Hades, Hestia, and Hera.

104. How is Demeter chiefly known in the mythical tales?

As the mother grieving for the loss of her child Persephonê.[1]

105. What was the cause of this sorrow?

Zeus, it is said, had, without the knowledge of Demeter, promised Hades that Persephonê should be his wife; and while the maiden was

---

[1] Tales of Ancient Greece. "The Sorrow of Demeter."

gathering flowers in the fields of Enna, the earth opened, and Hades, appearing in a chariot drawn by coal-black horses, took her away to his dark home.

106. How was this loss borne by Demeter?

She put on a dark mourning-robe, and, refusing to be comforted, wandered with a torch in her hand for nine days, and nights searching for her daughter.

107. Did she receive any aid in her search?

On the tenth day she met Hecate, who could not say where the maiden was, as she had only heard her cry when Hades seized her. Demeter then went to Helios, who sees all things, and from him she learnt that Persephonê was now queen of the dark realm beneath the earth.

108. Was Demeter satisfied with these tidings?

No. She refused to visit Olympus, and wandered over the earth, mourning and weeping for her child.

109. What was the effect of her grief and anger?

The husbandmen toiled in vain, for not a seed came up from the earth; not a blossom was seen upon the trees; and it seemed that all mortal things must soon die.

110. What was the end of her wanderings?

Roaming along in her great agony, she came at last to Eleusis, and sat down near a fountain, where she was kindly greeted by the daughters of King Keleos when they came to draw water, and at their entreaty she took up her abode in their house.

111. Was her grief now assuaged?

No. During her year's sojourn at Eleusis the earth still shared in the sorrow of Demeter, and yielded no fruits.

112. How did she recompense the kindness which she received in the house of Keleos?

On this subject more than one story is told. In one, it is said that she nursed Demophoon, the son of Keleos, and that under her care the child grew up glorious in beauty; that Demeter bathed him every day in fire, to render him immortal, but that his mother Metaneira, seeing him in the fiery bath, screamed with fear, and Demeter told her that but for her cries her son would have known neither old age nor death, whereas now he must grow old and die like other men.

113. What is the other tale?

According to this version, it is said that on the alarm given by Metaneira, Demeter suffered the child, Demophoon, to be consumed by flames, but, as an atonement for this, she gave to his brother, Triptolemus, a chariot drawn by winged dragons, and taught him how to plough the earth and to sow wheat.

114. How is the story of Demeter continued?

The terrible drought and famine caused by the anger of Demeter is said to have convinced Zeus that every thing on the earth must die unless her grief could be soothed; but as she would listen to no prayers until her child was brought back to her, Zeus at last sent Hermes, who returned with Persephonê from Hades.

115. Where did the meeting take place, and what followed it?

At Eleusis: and the grief of Demeter being now swallowed up in a deeper joy, the earth and all things in it shared her gladness, and peace and plenty returned to every land.

116. Did Persephonê remain altogether with Demeter?

No. Before Hermes took her away, Hades gave her some pomegranate seeds to eat, and she was thus bound to return to his dreary kingdom.

117. Did Demeter consent to this?

Not being able to keep her daughter always with her, she agreed that Persephonê should spend a certain portion of each year (some said four, others six months) with Hades.

118. What memorial is she said to have left of her presence at Eleusis?

Having bidden Keleos to build a temple for her worship, she taught him and his people the great Eleusinian mysteries, which were regularly celebrated there in her honor.

119. How was this legend regarded by the people of Eleusis?

As the history of events which had actually occurred at the place.

120. What was the origin of the legend?

It grew up out of the old phrases which had at first described the changes of summer and winter.

121. What, then, is Demeter?

She is the earth, who was called *the mother of all things*, and more particularly the mother of *the maiden* (Korê).

122. How did this furnish a groundwork for the later legend?

When the spring-time came, men had said, once, that the daughter of the Earth was returning in all her beauty; and when summer faded into winter, they said that the beautiful child had been stolen away from her mother by dark beings, who kept her imprisoned beneath the earth.

123. What, then, is the sorrow of Demeter?

The gloom which falls on the earth during the cheerless months of winter.

124. Is this story found in the legends of other nations?

Yes. It exists in many versions, especially in the legends of northern countries. In these Persephonê is a beautiful maiden, who, while the earth without is cold and dead, lies wrapped in slumber, hidden away from all mortal eyes.

125. Do these stories resemble the Greek tale in any other way?

Yes. As Demeter is the earth, which is full of mineral treasures as well as of fruit-giving seeds, the idea of wealth was connected with her name, and the loss of Persephonê was the taking away of her treasures. So in the Norse tales, the Niflungs (or the children of the mist) hide away the treasures of the earth, until they are compelled to yield them up again by one to whom they must submit, as Hades submits to the bidding of Hermes.

126. Where are Enna and Eleusis?

There is an Enna in Sicily and an Eleusis in Attica; but the Enna and Eleusis of the legend are names of the same kind as Delos, Lycia, and Ortygia, the land of light where Phœbus Apollo is born. The word Eleusis means a *coming* or an *approach*, and would naturally be applied to the return of spring after her absence during winter, and to the spot where the mother might be supposed to meet her child.

ATHENA, OR ATHENE.

127. Who was Athena?

The daughter of Zeus, who is said to have sprung from the forehead of her father, when, according to some poets, Hephæstus had split it open with an axe.

128. How is this strange tale to be explained?

By comparing the Greek with the Hindu tale, which gives it in an earlier form.

129. What does this comparison teach us?

That Athena is a name for the *Dawn*, who is in the Indian poems called Ahanâ and Dahanâ.

130. How does this explain her springing from the forehead of her father?

As Zeus was a name for the sky or heaven, so the Dawn was said to spring from the forehead of the sky—in other words, from the east.

131. What has this to do with the axe of Hephæstus?

This part of the story grew up out of an expression which had said only that the morning light opened or lit up the dark face or forehead of the sky.

132. What names were given to Athena, as having been so born?

She was called in some Greek States Koryphasia (from Koryphê, *a head*) and Akria (*topmost*), and by the Romans Capta (from caput, *the head*).

133. How was her name Tritogeneia explained?

By some it was thought to mean that she was born on the third day (from trita, *third*); but this explanation has no meaning. Others explained it by the word Trito, which in one Greek dialect meant a head; and others again said that she was so called as having been born on the banks of the Libyan lake Tritonis, or of the river Triton.

134. Are any of these explanations sufficient?

No. There were many rivers called Triton,

and hence we have to find out what is meant by the word Triton.

135. Can this be ascertained?

Yes. In the oldest Hindu or Sanskrit hymns we read of a god called Trita, who rules over the air and the waters. This Triton is really the same god as Dyu or Zeus, the sky; and hence Tritogeneia is the daughter of the sky— or, in other words, the morning.

136. What was the earliest office of Athena?

That of waking people from their slumbers: hence, next to the owl, the cock (the bird of the morning) is sacred to Athena.

137. But is not Athena also the goddess of wisdom?

Yes. As in the ancient language of India the same word which means *to wake* means also *to know*, so the goddess who made people wake was thought to be the goddess who made people to know.

138. Are there any variations in the legends of Athena?

Yes. According to some, she was a child, not of Zeus, but of the winged giant, Pallas, or of Poseidon, or Hephæstus. While others again speak of her as always a maiden, others say that Apollo was her son.

139. How is this to be explained?

As following the dawn, Apollo may be called the son of Athena; but if he is regarded as springing from the night, he is the son of Leto.

140. In what relation does she stand to Zeus?

Generally, in that of perfect harmony and submission.

141. What exceptions are there to this rule?

She shared in the conspiracy of Poseidon and Hera to dethrone or imprison Zeus, and she aided Prometheus in stealing fire from heaven against the will of Zeus. She is also said to have done this from a passionate love for Prometheus, whereas she is generally described as insensible to all such feelings.

142. Is Athena introduced into many legends?

She appears, throughout the Iliad, as the goddess who knows most deeply the mind of Zeus, and as the guide and comforter of Achilles, Odysseus, and other heroes.

143. Are there any stories in which she is described as acting from unworthy or unseemly motives?

In the legend of Pandora,[1] she takes part in the plot which results in increasing the misery of mankind.

144. What city bears the name of this goddess?

Athens, which is said to have been named

---

[1] Tales of Ancient Greece. "Epimetheus and Pandora."

after her when she produced the olive-tree as a better gift for man than the horse, which had been created by Poseidon, who wished the city to be called Poseidonia.

145. How is Athena represented?

As the goddess with the bright or gleaming eyes (Glaukopis), and as having on her ægis or cloak the face of the Gorgon Medusa, which turned all who looked on it into stone.

146. What celebrated temple was dedicated to her honor?

The Parthenon, on the Acropolis of Athens, before which stood the colossal statue of the goddess, carved in gold and ivory by the great sculptor Pheidias, the friend of Pericles (in the fifth century B. C.)

147. Was Athena known to the Romans and Latins?

Not under this name; but their goddess Minerva so nearly resembles her, that both may be regarded as the same deity.

148. What, then, are the points of difference between Athena and Minerva?

The idea of the Latin goddess is far higher than that of the Greek. The name Minerva is connected with the Latin word *mens*, which is the same as the Greek *ménos*, and the English *mind;* that of Athena conveys only the idea of outward, not of mental brightness.

ARES.

149. Who was Ares?

A son, according to some stories, of Zeus and Hera, and the god of the din and tumult of war.

150. Was he not the god of war itself?

Not strictly, unless war is to be regarded as a mere desire for fighting. No higher idea than this enters into the notion of Ares. He changes capriciously from one side to another, and even takes pleasure in plaguing men with sicknesses and epidemics.

151. Does the character of Ares stand high in Greek tradition?

No. He is frequently overcome, and when he is wounded, his roar is as loud as that of nine or ten thousand warriors. He is also noted chiefly by his huge size and his bodily strength; and when prostrate on the battle-field, his body was said to cover many roods of ground.

152. What is the origin of the name?

It comes from the same root with the name of the Latin god Mars, and the Maruts of Indian mythology, and means the grinder or crusher.

153. To what objects was this name first applied?

To the storms which throw heaven and earth into confusion; and hence the idea of Ares is confined to mere disorder and tumult.

154. With what goddess is the name of Ares chiefly connected?

With Aphroditê, whose love he is said to have obtained; but when she seemed to favor Adonis, Ares is described in some versions as changing himself into the boar which slew the youth of whom he was jealous.

155. What court at Athens bore the name of Ares?

That of Areiopagus, as being built on the Hill of Ares.

156. How did the hill receive this name?

It is said that Ares, having slain Halirrhothios, the son of Poseidon, was accused by the latter before the Olympian gods. Ares was acquitted, and the court was called after his name.

APHRODITE.

157. What is the generally received legend about the birth of Aphrodite?

It is said that she sprang from the bright foam of the sea, and was therefore called Aphrodite (Aphros, *froth*), and Anadyomene (*she who rises up*).

158. Whose daughter was she?

According to some tales, she was a child of Ouranos (*heaven*) and Hemera (*day*); but in the Iliad she is called the daughter of Zeus and Dione.

159. What, then, was Aphrodite originally?

A name for the dawn, as it rises from the sea in the east; and as the dawn is the most lovely of the sights of nature, Aphrodite became naturally to the Greek the goddess of beauty and love.

160. Does this agree with the legends of other countries?

Yes. In the oldest Vedic hymns of the Hindus the morning is called Duhitâ Divah, the daughter of Dyaus, just as Aphrodite is the daughter of Zeus.

161. What other name is given to the Morning in these hymns?

She is called Arjunî, the *bright* or *glistening*.

162. Is this name found in Greek mythology?

Yes. In the form Argynnis, who is described as a young woman beloved by Agamemnon.

163. How did this story spring up?

Because the real meaning of the word Argynnis had been forgotten, and only the idea of her beauty had been remembered. Argynnis therefore became to Agamemnon what Helen was to Menelaüs.

164. By whom was Aphrodite attended?

By the Horæ (or Hours), and more especially by the Charites, or Graces.

165. Are the Charites found in other legends besides the Greek?

In the Vedic hymns they are spoken of as the Harits, or horses of the dawn.

166. What is the meaning of the name?

It signifies brightness produced by anointing with fat or oil. This gave the idea of splendor, and so the horses of the dawn became, in the mind of the Greeks, the lovely attendants of Aphrodite.

167. Mention any other names of Aphrodite.

She was called Enalia and Pontia, both of which names mean that she belonged to the sea. She was also called Urania and Pandemos, or the goddess of pure, as well as gross and sensual love.

168. What does this show?

That the loveliness of the morning suggested the idea of tenderness and love, and that this idea passed into many shapes, according to the mind of the nations among whom these traditions came.

169. Was the worship of Aphrodite general?

It was found everywhere; but her most celebrated temples were in Cythera and Cyprus, in Cnidos, Paphos, and Corinth.

170. How was Aphrodite connected with the tale of the Trojan war?

APHRODITE.

At the marriage-feast of Peleus and Thetis, Eris (strife) threw down a golden apple to be given to the loveliest of the goddesses. The prize was claimed by Hera, Athena, and Aphrodite; and Zeus decreed that Paris, the son of Priam, should be judge. Paris gave it to Aphrodite, who tempted him to steal away Helen from Sparta; and this wrong done to Menelaüs, the husband of Helen, led to the Trojan war.

171. Who was the husband of Aphrodite?

In the Homeric poems, she is called the wife of Hephæstus :—the meaning of this being that the dawn is the bride of the light. She had also many lovers and many children; and the names, in most cases, explain themselves. As rising from the sea, she was loved by Poseidon; as stirring up a tumult of passion in the heart, she was loved by Ares, and became the mother of Deimos, Harmonia, and Eros (Fear, Harmony, and Love).

172. What other stories are told of her?

It is said that she loved Anchises, and became the mother of Æneas, the ancestor of Romulus. But she is more particularly known as the lover of Adonis.

173. Does the name Adonis belong to Greek mythology?

No. It is a Syrian or Hebrew word, signifying *Lord*.

174. Under what other name was Adonis worshipped in Syria?

Under that of Tammuz.[1]

175. What is the story of Adonis?

It is said that his great beauty charmed Aphrodite, but that he did not return her love; and that while yet in the spring-time of his youth he died from the bite of a wild boar, who tore his flesh with his tusk.

176. Is this tale like any other?

It resembles very many in which the hero dies young, or is smitten by a tusk, or spear, or thorn, or arrow. Thus in the Persian story, Isfendiyar is killed by a thorn thrown into his eye by Rustem; and in the Norse tales Sigurd is also killed by a lance, as Paris is slain by the poisoned arrows of Heracles.

177. What is the meaning of the tale of Aphrodite and Adonis?

The sorrow of Aphrodite for Adonis is the grief of Demeter for the loss of Persephone. In the latter, the earth mourns the departure of

---

[1] Ezekiel, viii. 14.

summer; in the former, the dawn or twilight is described as grieving for the death of the short-lived sun.

178. Do the stories about Aphrodite express any one idea?

No. She is represented in many ways, sometimes pure, sometimes gentle and loving, sometimes strong and vehement, sometimes indolent and listless, and sometimes as flushed with victory. In the temples of Sparta, she was represented as a conquering goddess in armor, just as later poets spoke of Eros (love) as being invincible in battle.

HEPHÆSTUS.

179. How is Hephæstus described?

As the smith of the gods, who forges irresistible weapons, but is lame and ugly.

180. Why is he thus described?

Because Hephæstus is, strictly, the brightness of flame, and as the flame comes from a little spark, so he was represented as puny and deformed at his birth, but as strong and powerful when grown up.

181. What stories are told of Hephæstus?

He is called the son of Zeus and Hera, but

sometimes of Hera only. His ugliness, it is said, so displeased his mother, that she wished to cast him out of Olympus; and when, afterward, he took her part in a quarrel, Zeus hurled him down from heaven, and he fell maimed and wounded in Lemnos, where he was kindly treated by the Sintians. Still he remained the cupbearer of the gods, while he also forged armor and weapons. Thus when the armor of Achilles had been taken by Hector from the body of Patroclus, Hephæstus, at the prayer of Thetis, made a new suit, which shone like the burnished sun, and bore him aloft like a bird upon the wing.

182. Who was the wife of Hephæstus?

In some versions Aphrodite, in others Charis, and in others again Aglaia,—all three meaning that the flame of fire is akin to the brightness of the sun's light.

183. Is Hephæstus found ir the traditions of other nations besides the Greeks?

Not under this name. By the Latins and Romans of later times he was known as Vulcan. In the Vedic poems he is called Agni, which is the same as the Latin word Ignis, fire.

184. In these traditions is he described in the same way?

In this and in other legends the Latins seem

to have borrowed many of the Greek notions; but the Hindu poets dwelt rather on the strength of the newly kindled flame than on its puniness, for, instead of saying, as we do, that fire burns and the wood smokes, they said, "Neighing like a horse that is greedy for food, it steps out from the strong prison; then the wind blows after his blast, and the path of Agni is dark at once."

185. Is the same idea found in the mythology of northern Europe?

Yes. In the story of Sigurd, who is the Achilles or Perseus of Norse legends, Regin, the smith of Hialprek, king of Denmark, answers precisely to Hephæstus, like whom he forges weapons which no enemy can withstand.

PHŒBUS APOLLO.

186. Who was Phœbus Apollo?

A son of Zeus and Leto.

187. Why was he so named?

He was called Phœbus, as being the god of light, and Apollo, a name explained by some as meaning the *destroyer*, because the sun's rays, when powerful, can destroy the life of animals and plants.

188. Is Phœbus, then, only a name for the sun?

It was nothing more at first; but in later times he was regarded as the god of light, who was not confined to his habitation in the sun. This was reserved for Helios, who stands to Phœbus in the relation of Nereus to Poseidon.

189. Why is Phœbus described as a son of Zeus and Leto?

He is called son of Zeus because the sun, like Athena, or the dawn, springs in the morning from the sky; and son of Leto because the night, as going before his rising, may be considered as the mother of the sun.

190. Does the name Leto reappear in any other form?

It is the same word as Lethe, the river which made men forget the past, and Latmos, the land of shadows, in which Endymion sleeps. The same root is seen also in the name of Leda, the mother of the twin Dioscuri.

191. What is the story of his birth?

It is said that Leto wandered through many lands, seeking in vain for a resting-place, and that at last she came to Delos, and said that if she could there have shelter, it should become glorious as the birthplace of Phœbus, and that men should come from all parts to enrich his holy temple with their gifts. Here, then, Phœbus was born, and at his birth the earth laughed beneath the smile of heaven, and Delos, though in itself a hard and stony land, covered itself with golden flowers. The nymphs wrapped him in a spotless robe, and when Themis fed him with nectar and ambrosia, the child took harp in hand, and proclaimed his office of declaring the will of Zeus to men.[1]

192. Why is he said to be born in Delos?

Because Delos means the *bright* land.

193. Do all the stories say that he was born in Delos?

No. He is called Lykegenes, as having been born in Lycia; and in some versions, Ortygia is mentioned as the birthplace both of Phœbus and of his sister Artemis.

194. Where are Lycia and Ortygia?

There was a Lycia in Asia, and an Ortygia near Ephesus, as well as in Sicily; but the Lycia and Ortygia of these legends must be sought in the beautiful Cloudland.

195. What is the meaning of the names?

Lycia is a word which, like Delos, means the land of light, and reappears in the Latin words lux, *light*, luceo, *to shine*, and Lucna or Luna, *the moon*. Ortygia is the land of the quail, which was said to be the earliest bird of spring; hence the quail-land became a name for the East, where the sun rises.

[1] Tales of Ancient Greece. "The Delian Apollo."

196. Did Phœbus remain long in Delos?

No. He soon left it to find his way westward to Pytho or Delphi.

197. Why did he so soon leave his birthplace?

Because the sun cannot linger in the east when he is risen; and so the poets sang how Apollo went from land to land, and how he loved the tall sea-cliffs and every jutting headland and the rivers which hasten to the broad sea, although he came back with ever fresh delight to his native Delos, as the sun reappears morning after morning, glorious as ever, in the east.

198. What change came over him soon after his birth?

At first he was swathed in golden bands, which denote the mild and gentle light of the newly risen sun; but presently he became the Chrysaor, or god of the golden sword, and his quiver was filled with arrows which never miss their mark.

199. Are these irresistible weapons given to other mythical heroes?

Yes. To Perseus, Theseus, Bellerophon, Heracles, Philoctetes, Achilles, Odysseus, Meleagros, Sigurd, Rustem, and many others.

200. What are the incidents of Apollo's journey to the Western Pytho?

Passing through many lands, he came to the fountain of Telphusa, where he wished to build himself a home; but Telphusa, saying that her broad plain could give him no peaceful abode, urged him to go on to the more favored land of Crisa. So Phœbus went on, and coming to Crisa, built himself a shrine beneath Mount Parnassus, and there slew the great dragon Python, who nursed Typhaon, the child of Hera.

201. What is this Python?

It is the great dragon or snake which appears in all solar legends. It is the Vritra of the Indian tale, the Echidna of the story of Heracles, the Sphinx in that of Œdipus, and the dragon Fafnir of the glistening heath in the tale of Sigurd.

202. Was the temple which Phœbus is said to have built at Delphi celebrated in after-times?

It was the greatest of all the oracles in Greece, and its fame was extended through all lands. When Xerxes invaded Greece, the force which he sent to plunder the sanctuary at Delphi is said to have been smitten by Phœbus Apollo, who hurled on them great rocks torn from the summit of Parnassus.

203. Who were the priests of this temple?

They are said to have been Cretans, whose ship Apollo, in the form of a glistening dolphin, guided round the Peloponnesus to the shores of Crisa, where the god came forth from the sea like a star, and filled the heavens with the brightness of his glory. Then having kindled on his altar the undying fire, he taught the Cretans the sacred rites of his worship, and charged them to deal truly and righteously with all who came with their offerings to his sanctuary.[1]

204. What other acts are attributed to Phœbus?

He is said to have been a lover of Daphne, who, to escape his pursuit, plunged into the waters of Peneius, her father.[2]

205. What is the meaning of this tale?

That Phœbus, as the sun-god, is a lover of the dawn, who is variously called Ahanâ, Dahanâ, Athena, and Daphne. The vanishing of Daphne in the stream is the disappearance of Eurydike (Eurydice) when Orpheus turns round too soon to look on her.

206. Are any more stories of this kind told about him?

He is said to have won the love of Coronis, the mother of his son Asklepios (Æsculapius),

---

[1] Tales of Ancient Greece. "The Pythian Apollo."
[2] Ibid. "Daphne."

and to have deserted her as Heracles leaves Iole, and Paris and Sigurd forsake Œnone and Brynhild.

207. How are these desertions to be explained?

As the sun, who may not tarry in his journey, may be said to forsake the fair and gentle dawn for the garish and flaunting noonday, so all the gods or heroes whose names were at first only names for the sun, are described as abandoning those to whom they had given their first love.

208. Is Apollo presented to us in any other aspects?

Yes; like Heracles, Perseus, and Bellerophon, he is compelled to toil for others without a recompense, as the sun was said to toil for the children of men against their will. Thus he has to serve for a year in the house of King Admetus.

209. Why is he called the father of Asklepios (Æsculapius)?

Because the sun's warmth can ward off diseases, or lessen pain and suffering, as well as inflict them.

210. By what other names is Apollo known?

He is called Hecatos and Hecaergos—names which signify the action of the sun's rays at a distance from the sun itself.

211. Are these names given to any other besides Phœbus?

Yes; Hecate, the moon, answers to Hecatos, just as Telephassa answers to Telephos.

212. Why is Apollo called the god of prophecy and wisdom?

As the rays of Helios penetrate all space and spy out all hidden things, the idea of wisdom was early connected with the name of the sun-god. Thus Apollo is said to know the mind of Zeus more intimately than any other of the gods, and although he may impart many secrets, there are others which he must never reveal.

213. Is he not also called the god of song and music?

Yes; but in the earliest form of the legend he is said to have acquired those gifts from Hermes, to whom they belonged by birthright.

214. Was the worship of Apollo common among the Greeks?

It was most widely spread, and had the greatest influence in forming the Greek character. Under the shadow of his temple at Delphi, the Amphictyonic council, the great religious association of the Greeks, held their meetings; and the answers given by the Delphian priestess are said to have changed more than once the current of Greek history.

ARTEMIS.

215. Who was Artemis?

A sister of Phœbus Apollo—according to some legends a twin sister, while according to others she was born before him.

216. How is she described?

As possessing almost all the powers of her brother, and exhibiting all his qualities. Thus, like him, she heals diseases and sends plagues, and, like him, she shoots arrows which never miss their mark.

217. What are the events in her history?

Properly speaking, Artemis has no mythical

history, although she is concerned in the fortunes of others. Thus she gives to Procris her hound and her resistless spear, and she heals Æneas when wounded in the Trojan war. She also sends the Calydonian boar as a requital for some affront which had been passed on her; and for the same reason she insists on the sacrifice of Iphigeneia, the daughter of Agamemnon.

218. What is the peculiarity of these tales?

That Atalanta, the maiden who first smites the Calydonian boar, is a counterpart of the virgin goddess; and that Iphigeneia, having been rescued from her doom, became a priestess in one of her temples, and was, in some places, worshipped as Artemis.

219. What was the birthplace of Artemis?

In some stories, Delos; in others, Ortygia— names which enter into the legends of Phœbus.

220. Was the idea attached to the name Artemis everywhere the same?

No; the idea of the Greek Artemis differs from that of the Ephesian Artemis, as much as the Syrian Adonis differs from the Greek Achilles.

HERMES.

221. What is the story of the birth of Hermes?

This son of Zeus and Maia is said to have been born early in the morning in a cave of the Kyllenian hill, and to have slumbered peacefully in his cradle for two or three hours, when stepping forth from the cave, he found a tortoise, which he killed, and with its shell he made a lyre by fastening sheepgut cords across it.[1]

222. What was his first exploit after making his lyre?

As the sun was going down he came to the

[1] Tales of Ancient Greece. "Hermes."

Pierian hills, where the cattle of Phœbus were feeding, and made ready to drive them back to Kyllene. Fearing that the tracks of the beasts on the sand might betray his theft, he drove them round about by crooked paths, so as to make it appear that they were going to the place from which they had been stolen, and his own feet he covered with tamarisk and myrtle leaves. As he passed, he saw an old man at work in a vineyard near Onchestos, and whispered into his ear a warning that he should take care not to remember too much of what he had seen. When the next morning dawned he had reached the stream of Alpheius, and there gathering logs of wood, he rubbed the pieces together till they burst into a flame. This was the first flame kindled on the earth, and so Hermes is called the giver of fire to mortal men.

223. How does the tale go on?

Hermes took two of the herd, and cut up their flesh into twelve portions, but he ate not the roasted meat, although he was sorely pressed by hunger. Then quenching the fire, he trampled down the ashes with all his might, and hastening on to Kyllene, darted into the cave through the keyhole of the door as softly as a summer breeze, and there lay like a babe, playing among the cradle-clothes with one hand, while his right hand held the tortoise lyre hidden beneath them.

224. Was the theft discovered?

When the morning dawned, Phœbus, coming to Onchestos, saw that his herds had been stolen. Meeting the old man at work in the vineyard, he asked if he knew who had taken them; but the man remembered the warning of Hermes, and could remember only that he had seen cattle moving, and a babe walking near them.

225. What did Phœbus do on hearing this?

Wrapped in a purple mist, he went to beautiful Pylos, and there came on the confused cattle-tracks, which he followed to the cave of Maia. Entering it, he found the babe Hermes asleep, and roughly waking him, demanded his cattle. The child pleaded his infancy. A babe of a day old cannot steal cattle, or even know what sort of things cows are. As Hermes gave this answer, his eyes winked slily, and he made a long, soft, whistling sound, as if the words of Phœbus had mightily amused him.

226. Did Phœbus take this excuse?

No. He caught up the child in his arms; but Hermes made so loud a noise that he quickly let him fall. Phœbus, taking this as a sign that he should find his cows, told Hermes to lead the way. Then Hermes, starting up in fear, pulled the cradle-clothes over his ears, and reproached Apollo for his cruelty. "I know nothing of cows," he said, "but their name. Zeus must decide the quarrel between us."

227. What was the judgment of Zeus?

When he had heard the complaint of Apollo, and listened to Hermes, who, winking his eyes and holding the clothes to his shoulders, protested that he knew not how to tell a lie, and that he could but play like other babes in his cradle, Zeus laughed, and bade Phœbus and the child be friends. Zeus then bowed his head. At that sign Hermes dared not disobey, and, hastening to the banks of Alpheius, he brought out the cattle from the folds where he had penned them.

228. Was the quarrel here ended?

No. Just at this moment Phœbus saw the spot where the fire had been kindled and the hides and bones of the slaughtered cattle, and wondering how a baby could flay whole cows, he seized him again and bound him with willow bands, which the child tore from his body like flax. Hermes, in his terror, thought upon his tortoise lyre, and called forth from it music so soft and soothing that Apollo, forgetting his anger, besought Hermes to teach him his wonderful art.

229. Did Hermes agree to this?

Yes. Hermes too envied the wisdom and hidden knowledge of Apollo, for Phœbus can see all things, even to the lowest depths of the green sea; and in return for this wisdom he promised to give him the lyre, which can discourse sweetly of all things, and drive away all care and sorrow. "Take it," he said, "for you know how to use it; but to those who touch it, not knowing how to draw forth its speech, it will babble strange nonsense, and rave with uncertain moanings."

230. Was this exchange made?

Only in part. It was not in the power of Phœbus to reveal the hidden secrets of years, but all that he could give to Hermes he gave. In his hands he placed a glittering scourge, and giving him charge over all his flocks and herds, bade him visit in their hidden dells and caves the hoary-headed Thriæ, which should teach him secrets hidden from all mortal men. In return for this, Hermes promised never to hurt the temple of Phœbus at Delphi.

231. Is it possible to explain this strange story?

On comparing it with the old Hindu or Vedic tales, we find that the name Hermes belongs to the same root with that of Saramâ; and that Saramâ is the dawn, as it creeps through the sky, peering about after the bright cows (the clouds) which have been stolen by the night, and hidden in its secret caves.

232. Is this name Saramâ found in any other forms?

Yes. It is proved to be the same name as *Helen*, whom Paris stole from Sparta. It comes from a root, *sar*, which means to creep, and it reappears in the names Erinys (the Vedic Saranyu) and Sarpedon, the son of Zeus, as well as in our word *serpent*, a creeping thing.

233. But how does the idea of Saramâ, or the Dawn, lead to that of the Greek Hermes?

In the hymns, Saramâ, when seeking after the cows, is said to go across the heavens with a soft breeze. She thus represents the morning, with the soft breath of summer winds whispering round her as she moves onward. In the minds of the Greeks, this idea of the breeze gradually shut out the idea of the morning, and so Hermes came to represent the wind, or air in motion.

234. Does this explain the story of Hermes?

Yes; even to its most minute features. The wind which whispers softly at its first rising, may freshen to a gale before it is an hour old, and sweep before it the clouds big with the rain that is to refresh the earth. It pries unseen into holes and crannies, it sweeps round dark corners, it plunges into glens and caves; and when people come out to see what mischief it has done, they hear its mocking laughter as it hastens on its way.

235. Whence comes the wit and humor of the tale?

In one sense, it was ready-made to the hands of the old Greek poets; but this may be said of every thing that has ever been done by man. We do but find out the things that exist; but only they who search patiently and truthfully can find them out; and the wit of the tale of Hermes sprang from this careful noting down of the varying action of the wind.

236. Is any one else said to have been the first to give fire to men?

Yes. Prometheus and Phoroneus. But Phoroneus, the Indian Bhuranyu, is only another name for fire ; and the story of Prometheus relates to fire brought down from heaven, while the fire kindled by Hermes is the fire produced in forests by the rubbing of branches in a high wind.

237. Why does not Hermes eat of the meat roasted by the fire which he has kindled?

Because, though the wind may cause the flame, it cannot itself consume that which the fire devours.

238. What is the return of Hermes to the cave in which he was born?

The dying down of the storm, until at last it is lulled to sleep.

239. To what does the defence of Hermes point?

To the seeming helplessness of the soft breeze, which, as we might fancy, could never grow into a hurricane.

240. How are we to explain the noise made by Hermes when Apollo seizes him in his arms?

It is a momentary blast of wind, which dies away as suddenly as it came.

241. What is the music of Hermes?

The melody of the winds, which can awake feelings of joy and sorrow, of regret and yearning, of fear and hope, of vehement gladness or utter despair.

242. Why does Phœbus refuse to impart his wisdom to Hermes?

Because the rays of the sun can go down far beneath the surface of the sea, and shoot out through the vast expanse of heaven, where the breath of the wind can never be felt.

243. What powers does Phœbus give him in return for his lyre?

He is made the guardian of the steeds of the Sun, and receives a scourge with which to drive them. In other words, the bright clouds must move across the sky when the wind drives them. He is also told that his music shall cheer and soothe the children of men, and that his breath shall waft the spirits of the dead to their unseen home.

244. What is the title of Hermes as the guide of the dead to the land of Hades?

He is the Psychopompos, the leader of souls.

245. Has he any other office?

He is the messenger of the gods, and especially of Zeus.

246. Why is Hermes bidden to go to the Thriæ for wisdom?

Because we may speak of the wind, when it pierces into caves and glens and all secret places, as seeking to discover the hidden treasures of the earth, and to gain a knowledge to which man can never attain.

247. Is Hermes, then, always the friend of man?

No. The poet ends the Homeric hymn by saying that his kindness to men is not equal to his love for the Sun, and that he has a way of doing them mischief while they sleep.

248. How is this to be explained?

Of sudden storms which may rise during the night; and as the mischief so done is wrought against their will, Hermes is called a thief and the prince of thieves, and Apollo foresees that he will break into many a house and set many a herdsman grieving for his cattle, to the end of time.

249. How is Hermes commonly represented?

With a staff in his hand, as the messenger of the gods and the guide of the dead, and with golden sandals which bear him as swiftly as a bird through the heavens. These sandals were placed on the feet of Perseus before he set out on his journey to slay the Gorgon Medusa.

DIONYSUS.

250. Who was Dionysus?

The god of the vine and its fruits.

251. Whose son was he said to be?

There is an almost endless number of versions for every incident in the history of this god. Some call him a son of Zeus or Demeter, or Io, or Dione. Others make him a son of Ammon and Amalthcia, the nurse of Zeus in the cave of Dicte. But the most popular version was that which made him a son of of Zeus and Semele, the daughter of Cadmus, king of Thebes.

252. Is there more than one story about his birth?

Yes. One tale relates that Cadmus, on learning that his daughter had become the mother of Dionysus, put her and her child in a chest, which the sea cast up on the shores of Brasiæ; Semele was taken up dead, but the babe was rescued and nourished by Ino. This incident is repeated in the story of Perseus and Danaë.

253. What other account is given of his birth?

It is said that Hera, being jealous of Semele, tempted her to her ruin. Semele, thus urged, asked Zeus to visit her in his Olympian splendor, and was scorched by the lightnings as he approached. In the midst of the blazing thunderbolts Dionysus was born, and Semele departed for a long sojourn in the land of Hades.[1]

254. Where was Dionysus brought up?

Some say in Naxos; others on Mount Nysa; but there were several mountains of this name, as there was more than one Ortygia and river Triton, where Phœbus and Athena were said to have been born.

255. What was the career of Dionysus?

Like Heracles, Perseus, Theseus, and all other heroes, he had to pass through a time of griev-

[1] Tales of Ancient Greece. "Semele."

ous toil and danger before he attained to fame and glory.

256. How were these hard tasks brought to an end?

Dionysus, it is said, resolved to leave Orchomenos, where he had spent his youth, and having journeyed to the sea, he stood on a jutting rock, where his dark locks streamed over his shoulders and his purple robe rustled in the breeze. The splendor of his form caught the eyes of some Tyrrhenians who were sailing by. Leaving their vessel, they came to the rock, and seizing Dionysus, bound him with strong withy bands, which fell from him like leaves from a tree in autumn. In vain the helmsman warned them to have nothing to do with one who belonged to the race of the undying gods; but as they sailed away with Dionysus, suddenly there ran over the deck a stream of purple wine, and a fragrance as of a heavenly banquet filled the air. Over the masts and sailyards a vine clambered; round the tackling tangled masses of ivy were mingled with bunches of glistening grapes, and bright garlands shone like jewels on every oarpin.[1]

257. What followed these wonders?

---

[1] Tales of Ancient Greece. "Dionysos."

The sailors, smitten with fear, crowded round the helmsman, when suddenly a loud roar was heard, and a tawny lion and a grisly bear stood fronting them. The men leaped over the ship's side, and were changed into dolphins; and Dionysus, once more taking his human form, rewarded the helmsman for his kindness, and brought a north wind which carried the ship to the land of Egypt, where Proteus was king.

258. Did Dionysus remain long in Egypt?

No. He journeyed now through many lands; through Ethiopia and India, and other countries, followed everywhere by crowds of women, who worshipped him with wild cries and songs. At last he returned to Thebes, where Cadmus had made his son Pentheus king.

259. How was Dionysus received by Pentheus?

With great suspicion, on account of the strange rites which he taught to the women, and the frenzy with which he inspired them.

260. Did Pentheus succeed in curing their madness?

No. Climbing into a tree to see their orgies, he was discovered by the women, who tore him to pieces, his own mother, Agavê, being the first to lay hands on him.[1]

[1] Tales of Ancient Greece. "Pentheus."

261. What other acts are recorded of Dionysus?

He is said to have brought back Semelê from Hades, and to have led her to Olympus, where she was known under the name Thyônê.

HERACLES.

262. Who was Heracles?

A son of Zeus and Alcmênê.

263. How may his life be generally described?

As a long servitude to a master meaner and weaker than himself, and as one continued sacrifice of himself for the good of others.

264. What is his chief characteristic?

An irresistible bodily strength, which is always used to help the weak and suffering and for the destruction of all noxious things.

265. What is the meaning of the name?

Like that of Hera, it signifies a solar deity.

266. How came it to pass that Heracles should be the servant of an unworthy master?

Zeus, it is said, boasted to Hera on the day on which Heracles was born that the child then to be born of the family of Perseus should be the mightiest of men. Hera, learning this, caused Eurystheus to be born before Heracles.

267. What was the origin of this tale?

It sprung from old phrases which had spoken of the sun as toiling for so poor and weak a creature as man.

268. Is the life of Heracles, then, only a summary of the daily or yearly course of the sun?

Yes. Every feature of the many legends connected with his name may be traced back to phrases which spoke of the sun as born to a life of toil, as entering on his weary tasks after a brief but happy infancy, and as sinking finally to his rest after a fierce battle with the clouds which had hindered his journey.

269. When did the labors of Heracles begin?

They may be said to have begun in his cradle. The toils known as the twelve labors of Heracles are assigned to later periods of life. But this number was fixed upon by the poets of a comparatively late age, who collected many local traditions, some based on facts, some purely fictitious, and ascribed them all to Heracles. The Homeric poets make no attempt to classify his toils or his exploits.

270. What is recorded of the infancy of Heracles?

It is said that as he lay sleeping in his cradle two snakes coiled themselves around him, and that the child on waking placed his hands round their necks, and gradually tightened his grasp until they fell dead upon the ground.[1]

271. What are these serpents?

They are the serpents of the night, or of darkness, on which the sun may be said to lay his hands when he rises, and which he slays as he climbs higher into the heavens.

272. In what country was Heracles born?

In Argos.

273. Why was he born there?

Because Argos is a word signifying *brightness*. Argos, therefore, is the same as Delos and Ortygia, the birthplace of Phœbus and his sister Artemis.

274. By whom was Heracles taught?

By the wise centaur Cheiron.

275. Who were the Centaurs?

---

[1] Tales of Ancient Greece. "The toils of Heracles."

Beings with the head of a man joined to the body of a horse.

276. Whence came this notion?

Apparently from the Indian phrases which spoke of the Gandharvas, or bright clouds, as riding along the sky.

277. How was the legend of Heracles treated by the sophist Prodicus?

As illustrating the victory of righteousness over iniquity.

278. How does he show this?

He represents Heracles as accosted by two maidens, one clad in a seemly robe of pure white, the other scantily clothed and with a flushed face and restless eyes. The latter, who is called Kakia, or Vice, tempts him with the offer of ease and pleasures; the other (Aretê, or Virtue) bids him toil manfully for a future and perhaps distant recompense. Heracles follows the counsel of Aretê, and begins his toils with a brave heart.

279. What maiden is said to have won the youthful love of Heracles?

Iolê, the daughter of Eurytus, king of Œchalia; but from her he was soon parted.

280. Why?

Because all the heroes who represent the sun

are always parted from their first love, just as the sun leaves the beautiful dawn behind him as he rises higher into the heaven.

281. What is the meaning of the name Iolê?

It signifies the *violet* color, and points to the violet-colored clouds which are seen only at sunrise or sunset.

282. Does this name appear in other legends?

Yes. In the forms of Iamos, Iolaos, and Iocaste.

283. Mention some of the chief exploits of Heracles.

He is said to have smitten the hundred-headed Hydra, or water-snake, of the lake of Lerna, the wild boar of Erymanthus, and the Harpies of the swamps of Stymphalus.

284. Do these exploits resemble those of other heroes?

Yes. They merely reproduce the slaying of Python by Phœbus, of Fafnir by Sigurd, of the Sphinx by Œdipus, of the Libyan dragon by Perseus, of the Minotaur by Theseus, and of Vritra by Indra.

285. What other deeds are recorded of him?

The gathering of the golden apples from the gardens of the Hesperides; in other words, the golden-colored clouds which are grouped round the sun as he sinks in the western sky.

286. What followed these great exploits?

He married Deianeira, the daughter of Œneus, chief of Calydon.

287. In what relation does Deianeira stand to Iolê?

In that of Helen to Œnone, in the story of Paris. In the same way Sigurd marries Gudrun after forsaking Brynhild; and Achilles, Odysseus, Theseus, and Kephalos are likewise parted from or abandon the women to whom they had plighted their troth.

288. Did Heracles remain with Deianeira during the rest of his life?

No. One day he smote Eunomus, the son of Œneus with his unerring spear, and then he could no longer be restrained from pursuing his westward journey.

289. Is the slaying of Eunomus like any incident in other tales?

It is only another form of the story which represents Tantalus as slaying his own son.

290. Did Deianeira leave her home with Heracles?

Yes. She went with him as far as Trachis, having received on the way from the centaur Nessus (whom Heracles slew) a shell filled with his blood.

291. What was the object of this gift?

Nessus said that by spreading it on a robe

for Heracles to wear, she might at any time regain his love if she should happen to lose it.

292. Did this come about?

Deianeira thought so: for, as she abode at Trachis, she heard of the capture of Œchalia by Heracles, and that he was bringing back with him the lovely maiden Iolê. She therefore sent him the robe annointed with the blood of Nessus.

293. Did Heracles put it on?

Yes. The messenger found him on the point of offering sacrifice; and Heracles put on the garment, which speedily burnt into his flesh, and made his blood rush in streams over the ground. Heracles bade them carry him to the top of Mount Œta, and there in the midst of a thunder-storm he died, gazing on Iolê who stood weeping by his side.

294. What is the meaning of this scene?

It is the last incident in what has been called the Tragedy of Nature—the battle of the sun with the clouds, which gather round him like mortal enemies, at his setting. As he sinks, the fiery mists embrace him, and the purple vapors rush across the sky, like the streams of blood which gush from the hero's body, while the violet-colored evening clouds seem to cheer him in his dying agony.

295. What are the weapons of Heracles?

He uses sometimes a club, sometimes a spear, and sometimes poisoned arrows.

296. Did the Greeks ever use poisoned arrows?

There is no evidence whatever of their ever having done so.

297. Do any other mythical heroes use such weapons?

Yes; Philoctetes and Odysseus.

298. How came such unmanly modes of warfare to be attributed by the Greeks to their greatest heroes?

Because the word *ios*, a spear, is the same in sound as the word *ios*, poison. Hence the two ideas were mingled together, and it was said that Helios, Heracles, and other heroes fought with poisoned arrows or lances.

299. Were the wanderings of Heracles confined to Greece?

No. He journeys over the whole world, but, like the sun, moves always from east to west.

300. Is the character of Heracles simply one of self-sacrifice or self-devotion?

No. If the sun may be spoken of as toiling for others, he may also be spoken of as enjoying in every land the fruits which he has ripened. Hence Heracles became a person fond of eating and drinking; and thus when in the house of Admetus he learns that his host has just lost his wife, he regards this as no reason why he should lose his dinner. The same burlesque spirit marks the conflict with Thanatos (or death), in which Heracles rescues Alkestis (Alcestis) from his grasp.

301. What is the story of Heracles and Echidna?

Wandering in Scythia, he is said to have met Echidna, who kept him in her cave for some time before she would let him depart.

302. Does this story resemble any other?

It has no features peculiar to itself. Heracles comes to her abode searching for his cattle which have been stolen, just as Phœbus searches for the cows stolen by Hermes, or as Indra seeks for the cows stolen by the Panis. The gloomy land in which the Echidna dwells, is simply the dreary country of the Graiæ which Perseus enters in his search for Medusa. The detention of Heracles in her cave denotes simply the time which passes between the setting of the sun and his rising. When he leaves Echidna, he gives her weapons which she is to yield up only to him who is able to use them—an incident which is repeated precisely in the legends of Theseus and Sigurd.

303. Is Heracles a hero peculiar to Greek mythology?

No. Under the same or other names we find a hero of this kind in the mythical legends of almost every country; but in all we have precisely the same kind of incidents, pointing to the old phrases which described the course of the sun from his rising to his setting.

PERSEUS.

304. Who was Perseus?

The great hero of Argos, and the mythical founder of the dynasty of the Perseidæ, or children of Perseus.

305. Did Heracles belong to the family of Perseus?

Yes; his mother Alcmene is described as a granddaughter of Perseus.

306. Why, then, has the story of Heracles been recounted before that of Perseus?

Because Heracles is a descendant of Perseus only in the mythology of Argos. Each state or city had its own store of traditions, none of which agreed on all points with those of other cities; and the legends of Heracles were far more widely known than those of Perseus, and furnished the groundwork not only for the history of Perseus but for that of many other heroes.

307. Is it meant by this that the story of Perseus is practically a repetition of that of Heracles?

Yes.

308. Were the people of Argos aware of this?

No. Differences in the names of the places and persons mentioned sufficiently disguised the points of agreement as to make them appear like different tales to those who were never led to examine them minutely and critically.

309. Had each city its own particular hero?

Almost all of them had some well-known hero as their defender. Thus Theseus at Athens and Œdipus at Thebes answered to Perseus at Argos.

310. How were the stories of these heroes regarded by the men of Argos, Thebes, and Athens?

As really distinct histories.

311. Are they so?

No: they are only a repetition of the same story, the names of places and persons being changed, and some few of the incidents altered.

312. What is the legend of the birth of Perseus?

It is said that Acrisios, king of Argos, was warned by the Delphian oracle that if his daughter Danae had a son, he would be slain by that child. So he shut her up in a dungeon, but Zeus entered it in the form of a golden shower, and Danae became the mother of Perseus. Acrisios then placed Danae and her babe in a chest which the waves of the sea carried to the island of Seriphos. There she with her child was rescued and kindly treated by Dictys, the brother of Polydectes, king of the island.[1]

313. How did Perseus grow up?

With more than human beauty and strength. His gleaming eyes and golden hair made him, like Phœbus, the lord of light.

314. What was the destined lot of Perseus?

One of hard toil and terrible danger, to be followed by a great reward.

315. How were his toils caused?

The cruel king Polydectes sought to win the love of Danae, and as Danae shrank from him, Polydectes shut her up in prison, saying that she should never come out of it until Perseus brought back the head of the Gorgon Medusa.

316. Who was Medusa?

One of the three Gorgons, the daughters of Phorcos and Keto. Medusa was mortal, but her sisters Stheino and Eurualê were immortal.

317. What is the story told about her?

She is said to have lived with her sisters in the distant west, far beyond the gardens of the Hesperides, where the sun never shone, and where no living thing was to be seen. Yearning for human love and sympathy, she visited her

---

[1] Tales of Ancient Greece. "Danae."

kinsfolk the Graiæ, but they would give her no help. So when Athena came from the Libyan land, Medusa besought her aid; but Athena refused it, saying that men would shrink from the dark countenance of the Gorgon; and when Medusa said that in the light of the sun her face might be as fair as that of Athena, the goddess in her anger told her that henceforth all mortal things which might look upon her face should be turned into stone. Thus her countenance was changed, and her hair was turned into snakes which coiled and twisted themselves round her temples [1]

318. How was Perseus enabled to find the home of Medusa, and to slay her?

The gods came to his aid. When Perseus slept once more upon Argive soil, Athena stood before him, and gave him a mirror in which he might see the face of Medusa reflected, and thus know where to strike, for upon Medusa herself he could not gaze and live. When he awoke, he saw the mirror by his side, and knew that it was not a dream. So with a good hope he journeyed westward, and on the following night he saw in his sleep Hermes, the messenger of the gods, who gave him the sword which

---

[1] Tales of Ancient Greece. "Medusa."

slays all mortal things on which it may fall, and who bade him obtain the aid of the Graiæ in his further search. When he woke he took up the sword, and went to the land of the Graiæ, where Atlas bears up the pillars of the high heaven. There, in a cave, he found the three sisters, who had but one eye between them, which they passed from one to the other. This eye Perseus seized, and thus compelled the Graiæ to guide him to the dwelling of Medusa. By their advice he went to the banks of the ocean-stream which flows round all the earth, and there the nymphs gave him the helmet of Hades, which enables the wearer to move unseen, and a bag into which he was to put Medusa's head, and the golden sandals of Hermes, which should bear him swifter than a dream from the pursuit of the Gorgon sisters. Thus armed, Perseus drew nigh to the dwelling of the Gorgons, and then, while the three sisters slept, the unerring sword fell, and the woeful life of Medusa was ended.[1]

319. What was the history of Perseus after the death of Medusa?

When the immortal Gorgons awoke and saw their sister slain, they rushed in mad pursuit

---
[1] Tales of Ancient Greece. "Perseus."

after Perseus; but with the cap of Hades he went unseen, and the golden sandals bore him like a bird through the air. Onward he went until he heard a voice asking him whether he had brought with him the head of Medusa. It was the voice of the old man, Atlas, who bore up the pillars of heaven on his shoulders, and who longed to be released from his fearful labor. On his entreaty, Perseus showed him the Gorgon's face, and his rugged limbs soon grew stiff as ridges on a hill-side, and his streaming hair looked like the snow which covers a mountain summit. Thence Perseus rose into the land of the Hyperboreans, who know neither day nor night, nor storm, nor sickness, nor death, but live joyously among beautiful gardens where the flowers never fade away.

320. Did Perseus stay long in this happy land?

No: he remembered his mother Danae, in her prison-house at Seriphos, and once more, on his winged sandals, he flew to the Libyan shore, where on a rock he saw a fair maiden chained, while a great dragon approached to devour her. But before he seized his prey, the unerring sword smote him, and taking off his cap, Perseus stood before Andromeda; and soon after there was a marriage-feast, where the maiden sat as the bride of Perseus.[1]

321. What happened at this feast?

Phineus, who had wished to marry Andromeda, reviled Perseus, who, unveiling the Gorgon's face, turned Phineus and all his followers into stone.

322. Did Perseus remain in Libya?

Kepheus, the father of Andromeda, besought him to stay, but he hastened to Seriphos, where he delivered his mother Danae from her prison, and, with the Gorgon's face, turned into stone the tyrant Polydectes. Thus his work was done, and Perseus now gave back to Hermes the helmet of Hades and the sword and sandals, and Athena took the Gorgon's head and placed it upon her ægis.

323. Did Perseus then, after all, fulfil the warning given by the Delphian oracle to King Acrisios?

Yes. When, with Danae, he returned to Argos, Acrisios in great fear fled away to Larissa, where he was received by the chieftain Teutamidas. Thither also came Perseus, to take part in the great games to be held on the plain before the city. In these games Perseus was

[1] Tales of Ancient Greece. "Andromeda."

throughout the conqueror; but while he was throwing quoits, one turned aside and killed Acrisios.[1]

324. How was the life of Perseus ended?

Some said that grief at the death he had unwittingly caused led him to yield up to his kinsman Megapenthes the sovereignty of Argos, and that he went and died in the city of Tiryns, which he had surrounded with huge walls.

325. What stories does this legend chiefly resemble?

Those of Heracles, Theseus, Bellerophon, Kephalos, and Œdipus.

326. Is the warning given to Acrisios found in other tales?

Yes; Laios is warned at Thebes that he should be slain by his son; Priam, at Troy, is warned that his child will bring ruin on Ilion. The same warning is given also to the parents of Telephus, Cyrus, Romulus, and many others.

327. What follows the warning?

The children are exposed, some on a hillside, as Œdipus, Paris, and Telephus; some in chests on the sea, as Dionysus and Perseus; or in a cradle on a river's bank, as Romulus.

[1] Tales of Ancient Greece. "Acrisios."

In each case they are rescued, and their growth to manhood is generally described in the same way.

328. What is the golden shower in the prison of Danae?

The light of morning, which streams in upon the darkness of night.

329. What is the subjection of Perseus to Polydectes?

Another form of the subjection of Heracles to Eurystheus, of Poseidon to Laomedon, and of Apollo to Admetus.

330. Who is Polydectes?

The same as Polydegmon, or Hades, the king of the dark land, who greedily seizes all that comes within his grasp.

331. What are Medusa and her sisters?

Medusa is the starlit night, solemn in its beauty, and doomed to die when the sun rises; her sisters represent the absolute darkness which it was supposed that the sun could not penetrate.

332. What is the journey of Perseus to the land of the Graiæ?

The counterpart of the journey of Heracles to the land of the Hesperides.

333. What are the Graiæ?

They represent the twilight or gloaming; the region of doubtful shadows and dim mists.

334. What is the Libyan dragon slain by Perseus?

Another form of Python, Fafnir, Vritra, Sphinx, and the Chimæra.

335. How does the marriage of Andromeda resemble those of other mythical heroines?

It follows the slaughter of a monster, like that of Ariadne, Brynhild, Deianeira, Medeia, Jocasta, and others.

336. What is the return of Danae to Argos?

It is the restoration of Iole to Heracles, of Briseis to Achilles, of Antigone to Œdipus, and of Brynhild to Sigurd.

337. What is the sword which Perseus bears?

The piercing rays of the sun, which is invincible in its strength.

338. What other mythical beings have these irresistible weapons?

All those heroes whose lives in other respects resemble those of Heracles and Phœbus. Thus no others can wield the spear of Achilles or the bow of Odysseus; and the arrows of Heracles and Philoctetes are winged with death.

339. What is the meaning of the name Perseus?

It means the destroyer. Many of the heroes

have names from the monsters which they slay, as Bellerophontes, the slayer of Belleros, and Argeiphontes, the slayer of Argos Panoptes (the all-seeing).

340. What do these points of close resemblance show us?

That Perseus, Bellerophon, Heracles, Theseus, Achilles, Apollo, Odysseus, Sigurd, Rustem, and a host of others, are only different forms of one and the same person, and that the idea of this person has grown out of phrases which described originally the course of the sun in its daily or yearly round.

THESEUS.

341. Who was Theseus?

The great hero of Athens, corresponding to Perseus at Argos and Œdipus at Thebes.

342. Who are his parents?

His father is Ægeus and his mother is Æthra (the pure air).

343. Where was his youth passed?

At Trœzen, where he was to remain until he should be able to lift a great stone, under which his father had placed his sword and sandals.[1]

344. What are these sandals and this sword?

The sandals are the same as those of Hermes; the sword is that of Apollo Chrysaor, and corresponds to the arrows of Phœbus and Odysseus, and the spear of Achilles.

345. Is the way in which Theseus has to win them repeated in any other story?

Yes; in the story of Heracles and Echidna, and in the tale which afterward grew up into the Lay of the Nibelungs, or children of the mist (the Nibelungen Lied). Odin driving to

---

[1] Tales of Ancient Greece. "Theseus."

its hilt in an oak trunk the sword Gram, leaves it for the man who should be able to draw it out. It is drawn out by Sigmund, and when afterward broken, it is forged afresh for Sigurd by Regin, the smith, who corresponds to Hephæstus.

346. On gaining this sword, what exploits did Theseus perform?

Among other feats, he slays the giant Periphetes, the robber Sinis, the sow of Crommyon, and the cruel Procrustes, who tortured his victims by stretching their limbs until they died.

347. Did these exploits save him from further labors?

No. Like Perseus and Heracles, Theseus is doomed to a life of toil; and from Athens he was sent with the ship which bore the tribute children to be devoured by the Minotauros.

348. What was the Minotauros?

A monster in the form of a bull, which was said to be born from Pasiphaê, the wife of Minos.

349. How is this explained?

The name Pasiphaê denotes "one who gives light to all;" and the bull in the oldest Vedic hymns is constantly mentioned in connection with the sun and the chariot of Indra and Dahana. Europa also is borne across the sea on a spotless white bull. The distortion of the idea was caused by the forgetting that Pasiphaê, like Telephassa and Argynnis, was only a name for the morning.

350. What was the abode of the Minotauros?

The labyrinth of Crete.

351. What is this labyrinth?

It is the same as the bridal chamber which was wrought by Odysseus for Penelope. It reappears also in the maze of the Hyperborean gardens, which the sun lays out for his bride, the dawn.

352. How did Theseus fare on his errand?

By the help of Ariadne, the daughter of Minos, he slew the Minotaur; just as with the help of Medea, Jason slew the fire-breathing bulls of Colchis.

353. What became of Ariadne?

Theseus took her as far as Naxos, and there deserted her; but Dionysus came and made her his wife, and placed her abode in the constellation which is called Ariadne's crown.

354. Was Medea also deserted like Ariadne?

Yes; Jason forsook her to marry Glauke (the bright one), the daughter of King Creon.

But this desertion is simply the abandonment of Iole by Heracles, of Œnone by Paris, and of Brynhild by Sigurd; and it means only that the sun may not tarry with the dawn in the east.

355. What other incidents belong to the life of Theseus?

Like Œdipus and Perseus, he is said to have been the unwilling cause of his father's death, by neglecting to draw down the black sail which was spread only for the voyage to Crete. He is said also to have taken part in the Calydonian boar-hunt and in the voyage of the Argonauts, and to have brought up Persephonê from Hades.

356. How was Theseus regarded at Athens?

As the founder of the state, it is said that he brought all the townships (or demi) of Attica into one community, with Athens as their city. But in fact, the Athenians, looking on him as a real man, gradually made out his life to have been like the life of real men, by leaving out of sight the marvellous tales which were told about him. Some even said that the slayer of the Minotaur was not the same as the founder of the Athenian commonwealth; but they had no more warrant for so saying than others had for stripping the story of Theseus, the son of Æthra, of all its wonderful incidents.

ŒDIPUS.

357. Who was Œdipus?

The great hero of Thebes, in Bœotia, corresponding to Perseus at Argos and to Theseus at Athens.

358. What is the story of his birth and infancy?

His father Laios is said to have received from the oracle at Delphi the same warning which was given to Acrisios. Œdipus was therefore exposed immediately after his birth on the side of the hill of Kithairon (Cithæron); but some said that, like Dionysus and Perseus, he was placed in a chest, which was cast into the sea. Like them he was rescued, and taken to Corinth, where he passed as the son of Polybus and Merope.

359. How was the warning of the oracle fulfilled?

Journeying from Corinth to Thebes, Œdipus met on the road an old man in a chariot, and was ordered to get out of the way. On his refusal, the old man struck him, and was instantly slain by Œdipus.

[1] Tales of Ancient Greece (in division devoted to "Tales of Thebes"), "Laios."

360. In what condition did Œdipus find the Thebans?

In great distress from drought and sickness caused by the Sphinx, who, sitting on the brow of the hill over the city, uttered dark riddles, and who could not be overcome except by one who should expound them.¹

361. How did Œdipus save the city?

He solved the dark sayings of the Sphinx, who threw herself with a wild roar from the cliffs, and the parched soil was refreshed with abundant rain.

362. What was the reward of Œdipus?

It had been proclaimed that whoever should deliver the city from the Sphinx should marry the beautiful Iocastê, who was the mother of Œdipus.

363. Did this marriage take place?

Yes; for Œdipus knew not who his parents were; but the Erinys, who takes vengeance for murder, brought a plague on the city for the death of Laios, and the Delphian oracle charged them to get rid of the guilty man. When, after long search, it turned out that Œdipus had slain him, and that he was married to his own mother, he tore out his eyes, that he might not see the

---

[1] Tales of Ancient Greece (in division devoted to "Tales of Thebes,") "Œdipus."

misery which he had wrought, and Iocastê died in her bridal chamber.

364. Was this the end of these terrible evils?

No. Atê, who visits the sins of fathers on their children, had not yet done her work. Œdipus wandered forth from Thebes, a wretched exile, led by his daughter Antigone; and his sons, Eteocles and Polyneikes,¹ quarrelled for the sovereignty of Thebes, and waged a civil war, in which they met and slew each other.

365. What was the fate of Œdipus?

Coming at length to the grove of the Eumenides, near Athens, he received from Zeus warning that his death was near at hand; and sending for Theseus, he told him that Athens should be great and powerful, so long as none knew where Œdipus lay buried.² So, amid the flashing lightnings and the pealing of the thunder, Œdipus rested from his toil and trouble, cheered to the last hour by the tender love of Antigone.

366. What is the origin of this story?

It grew up in part from that idea of toil for the benefit of others, which marks the stories of

---

¹ Tales of Ancient Greece, (in division devoted to "Tales of Thebes,") "Polyneikes."
² Ib "Antigone."

Heracles, Perseus, Theseus, Bellerophon, and many others, and partly from old phrases which had spoken of the sun as having been united in the evening to the mother from whom he had sprung in the morning.

367. Where did the story probably end at first?

With the marriage of Œdipus to Iocastê, just as in the Sanskrit hymns Indra is called the husband of the Dawn, and sometimes her son.

368. How could he be called both her husband and her son?

As the dawn comes before the sun rises, Indra would be the child of Dahana: as being seen by her side, he might be called her husband. In fact, the whole nature of the gods in these very ancient poems is still transparent. "There are no genealogies, or settled marriages between the gods and goddesses. The father is sometimes the son, the brother is the husband, and she, who in one hymn is the mother, is in another the wife."

369. How is it that the latter part of the story of Œdipus did not grow up in India?

Because there the real meaning of such names as Œdipus and Iocaste was not forgotten. But to the Greeks, who thought that Œdipus and Iocaste were human beings, the idea of marriage between them was shocking, and the horrors which followed were very naturally invented.

370. But Œdipus is described as hurried on by a power which he cannot resist. How is this?

The sun cannot pause in his journey—he has no free action, and he must be united in the evening with the dawn from whom he had been parted in the morning. This notion, when applied to human actions, grew up into the idea of Necessity, called by the GreeksAnanke, or of Destiny, which they called Moira.

371. What is the meaning of the word Moira?

It means literally a portion; and in Homer, Moira is the being who assigns to men their lot in life, strictly under subjection to Zeus. But in later poems, she becomes mightier than Zeus and all the gods; and according to some versions there were three sisters, called Mœræ, or Fates, namely, Clotho, she who spins the thread of life, Lachesis, she who draws it out as she wills, and Atropos, the inexorable being who cuts it.

372. The deadly quarrels of the sons of Œdipus are traced to the working of Atê. What was Atê?

The word means "Mischievous Folly;" and in the Homeric poems Atê is nothing more. As such, Zeus hurls her out of heaven for causing

Eurystheus to be born before Heracles. But in later times, Atê became a fate or doom, resting on a house, after the shedding of innocent blood.

373. What is Iocaste?

Like Iole and Iamos, the word denotes the violet color, and meant at first the delicate tints of the morning clouds, or of the morning itself.

374. What is Laios?

Laios represents the darkness from which the sun springs, and answers to Leto the mother of Phœbus. The word is the same as the Indian Dasyu, an enemy, a name frequently applied to Vritra, the enemy of Indra.

375. What is the meaning of the word Œdipus?

Some thought that it was taken from words which meant "a man with swollen feet;" others fancied that it meant "the man who knew the riddle of the feet," because the Sphinx is said to have asked, "What creature goes on four feet in the morning, on two during the day, and on three in the evening?"

376. Are either of these notions correct?

The origin of this name is not known with certainty. It may come from the verbs which mean *to swell* or *to know;* but the two modes of accounting for it just mentioned are fancies of a later time.

377. What is meant by the exposure of Œdipus?

The notion sprung from a phrase which had said originally, 'The rays of the sun at its birth rest level on the earth, or on the hill-side.' Thus Paris is exposed on Idâ; but Idâ in the old Vedic poems is a name of the earth, who is called the wife of Dyaus or the sky. Idâ and Dyaus answer therefore to the Greek Ouranos and Gaia.

378. What is the Sphinx?

A creature who imprisons the rain in the clouds, and so causes a drought.

379. What is the meaning of the word?

It means one *who binds fast* (from the Greek word sphingo); the Sphinx, therefore, answers exactly to Ahi, or Echidna, the throttling serpent of darkness.

380. But was not the idea of the Sphinx derived from Egypt; and must not Sphinx therefore be an Egyptian word?

This was the mistaken notion of later times The Greeks had the idea and the name of the Sphinx (who was also called Phix, from a word connected with the Latin figo, *to fix*) ages before Egypt was thrown open to Greek merchants or travellers. The Greek Sphinx has the head of a woman with the body of a beast, the claws of a lion, the wings of a bird, and a serpent's tail, and might be represented in any attitude; but when Greeks came into Egypt, and found figures with a woman's head joined to a lion's body, they called them by the same name, and afterward fancied that they got the idea itself from the Egyptians.

381. Whence comes the notion of the Sphinx's riddle?

It was suggested by the mutterings and rumblings of the thunder, which men cannot understand.

382. Why should Œdipus understand it?

Because he has that wisdom of Phœbus (the god of light) which Hermes also sought to obtain.

383. What is the death of the Sphinx?

It is the victory of Indra who smites his enemy Vritra, and immediately brings rain on the thirsting earth. So the rain pours down on Thebes as soon as the Sphinx hurls herself from the cliff.

384. Under what form does the Sphinx appear in other stories?

As we have seen already, it is the same as

the Python and Fafnir: and it reappears also in Typhon and Polyphemus.

385. Where does Œdipus die?

In the sacred grove of the Eumenides.

386. Who are the Eumenides?

The Eumenides (a word which means literally 'the gentle beings,') are the same as the Erynyes (Allecto, the *implacable*, Megæra, *the envious*, and Tisiphone, *the avenger of blood*), commonly known as the Furies. The name Eumenides was used in order to avert their wrath.

387. Does the word Erinys, then, mean a Fury?

No. The name is one which cannot be explained in Greek; but it is the same word as the Indian Saranyû, which is the name for the dawn.

388. How came the lovely Saranyû, or morning, to be changed into the gloomy Erinys of the Greek?

So long as the meaning of the name was remembered, men had said of wicked doers, 'Saranyû will find out your sin,'" meaning that the light would discover their wickedness. Hence the Erinys was first the being who brought evil deeds to light, and was represented afterward in gloomy and fearful colors as their avenger.

389. What then is the death of Œdipus?

It is the death of the Sun in the beautiful groves of the dawn, which are otherwise called the gardens of the Hyperboreans, and which represent the fairy network of clouds which are the first to receive and the last to lose the light of the sun in the morning and the evening. Hence, although Œdipus dies in a thunderstorm, yet the Eumenides are kind to him, and his last hour is one of deep peace and tranquillity.

390. Which of his children remained to the last with Œdipus?

Antigone, whose name denotes the pale light which is born, or springs up, opposite to the sun at his setting.

391. What became of Antigone?

When the two sons of Œdipus slew each other, the body of Polyneikes was cast forth unburied, and in defiance of the commands of Creon, Antigone buried it. Creon, therefore, ordered her to be buried alive; and when Hæmon his son found her dead, he slew himself over her body.

PROCRIS.

392. Who was Procris?

A daughter of Erechtheus (a mythical king of Athens) and Herse.

393. How is Erechtheus described?

Erechtheus or Erichthonios (for the names are the same) is called a son of Hephæstus and Gê (the earth). He was born in the form of a serpent, and brought up by Athena.

394. What is the legend of Procris?

Procris, a being of marvellous beauty, won the love of Kephalos (Cephalus) who found her on mount Hymettus, when he came from the white shore of Eubœa. But Eos became jealous, when she saw Procris wedded to Kephalos; and she tempted Kephalos to doubt her faith. Kephalos going away, returned disguised (as Sigurd in the Volsung tale returns to Brynhild), and won the love of Procris in his altered form. Procris discovering the trick, fled away to Crete, and there dwelt in deep sorrow, until at length she was visited by Artemis, who gave her the spear which never missed its mark, and the dog who never failed to track his prey. So with the hound and spear, Procris came back to Athens, and was there the first always in the chase. Kephalos, filled with envy at her success, begged for the spear and dog, but Procris refused to give them except in return for his love. This Kephalos gave, and immediately discovered that it was his first wife Procris who stood before him. Fearing still the jealousy of Eos, Procris kept near Kephalos in the chase, until his spear smote her while she lay hidden in a thicket. Bitterly grieving at her death, Kephalos left Athens, and aided Amphitryon in ridding his land of noxious beasts; then journeying westward, he reached the Leucadian cape, where his strength failed him, and he fell into the sea.[1]

395. What is the origin of this story?

It sprung from three simple phrases, one of which said, "The sun loves the dew;" while the second said that "the morning loves the sun;" and the third added that "the sun kills the dew."

396. How is this proved?

Because Procris is called the child of Herse, a word which, even in Greek, means *dew*, and

---

[1] Tales of Ancient Greece. "Kephalos and Procris."

because the name Procris itself comes from a Sanskrit word meaning *to sprinkle*. Eos, again, is the goddess of the east, or morning; and Kephalos is a word meaning the head of the sun.

397. How did this suggest the details of the story?

As the sun looks on the dew early in the morning, so Kephalos wins the love of Procris in early youth, while the love of the dawn for the sun is changed into the jealousy of Eos for Procris. But each dewdrop reflects the sun, and Procris was thus said to grant her love to a Kephalos who, though changed, is still the same. She is smitten by the spear of Artemis, which represents the rays of the sun as it gains strength and dries up the dew. Kephalos causes her death against his will while she lingers in a thicket (a place where the dew lingers longest), just as Phœbus loses Daphne and Orpheus is parted from Eurydike. Having slain his bride, Kephalos must journey westward, like Heracles, Perseus, and other heroes. Like them he toils for others, and like them he dies in the far west after his work is done.

398. Who was Orpheus?

He is generally called a son of the river Œagros and the muse Calliope.

399. What is the common story of Orpheus?

He is said to have won the love of the beautiful Eurydikê (Eurydice), who died soon after from the bite of a snake. Orpheus, wretched at her loss, had no longer the heart to wake from his golden lyre the music which made men, beasts, and trees follow him in delight. He determined, therefore, to seek Eurydike in the land of the dead, and having soothed the dog of Hades (Kerberos or Cerberus) with his song, he was brought before Polydegmon and Persephone, who suffered him to lead his wife away, on condition that he should not look on her face till she had reached the earth. Orpheus, forgetting his promise, looked round too soon, and Eurydike was torn away from him almost before he could see her. The grief of Orpheus again silenced his music, until he died on the banks of the Hebrus.[1]

[1] Tales of Ancient Greece. "Orpheus and Eurydike."

ORPHEUS. 139

400. What is the name of Orpheus?

It is the same as the Indian Ribhu, a name that seems at a very early period to have been applied to the sun. In the Veda it is applied to many deities. In its original sense it seems to have denoted creative power or energy. In the opinion of some, Orpheus represents the winds, who tear up the trees as they course along, chanting their wild music.

401. Is there, then, a mingling of two notions in the story?

Yes; the idea of the morning, with its short-lived beauty, is confused, as in the story of Hermes, with the idea of the breeze which generally accompanies the dawn.

402. Does the name Eurydike resemble any others?

It comes from the same word from which have been formed such names as Europa, Eurytos, Euryphassa, and many others, all denoting the broad-spreading flush of the dawn across the sky.

403. What is the snake which bites Eurydike?

The serpent of darkness, which kills the beautiful twilight in the evening.

404. What is the pilgrimage of Orpheus?

The journey which during the hours of night the sun was supposed to take in order to bring back the dawn in the morning, which he does only to destroy her with his dazzling splendor.

405. What, then, is the final departure of Eurydike?

It is another form of the deaths of Daphne and Procris.

EUROPA.

406. Who was Europa?

According to the common story, a daughter of Agenor and Telephassa, and a sister of Cadmus and Phœnix.

407. Where was she born?

In Phœnicia, whence in her early youth she was carried away by Zeus, in the form of a white bull.[1]

408. Whither did the bull carry her?

To Delphi.

409. What is the sequel of the story?

Agenor ordered his sons to go in search of their sister, and Telephassa, going with them, journeyed westward until they came to Thessaly. There Telephassa grew faint and died, and Cadmus going on met Phœbus, who told him that he should hear tidings of his sister at Delphi, and that after he had found her he should follow a cow, who would lead him to the spot where he was to build a city. Having thus found his sister, he left Delphi; and as they

---

[1] Tales of Ancient Greece. "Cadmus and Europa."

passed along, a cow rose up and went before them, lying down to rest only when they reached the spot where Cadmus built the city called Thebes.

410. What was the after-life of Cadmus?

He first smote the dragon near the well of Ares, and then, after a year of further toil, received Harmonia as his wife from Zeus. Cadmus and Harmonia became the parents of Ino, Semele, and Agave, and were finally taken away by Zeus into Elysium, or the paradise of the good.

411. What is the meaning of the name Europa?

Like Euryphassa, Eurynome, and very many others, it expresses the broad-spreading light of the dawn, which is carried from east to west by Zeus (Dyaus, the sky), represented in the oldest poems under the form of a bull.

412. Do the other names also explain themselves?

Phœnicia, where she is born, is the purple land of morning, like the Delos, Lycia, and Ortygia where Phœbus and Artemis spring to life. Her brother Phœnix is the teacher of the great hero, Achilles, the lover of Briseis (Brisaya); and Telephassa (she who shines from far) is, like Telephos and Telemachus, a name of the dawn light, which, shooting across the sky, dies out in the west. The name Cadmus has been identified with the Syrian word Kedem, the *east*, and is thus a name for the sun god. Like Phœbus, Theseus, and Œdipus, he slays monsters, and then, like them, receives a fair bride as his reward.

413. How was this story regarded in later times?

As furnishing evidence that Bœotia was colonized from the Syrian Phœnicia; but of this fact the proof is scarcely adequate, and in any case it cannot be derived from this legend.

MELEAGROS (MELEAGER).

414. Who was Meleagros?

A son of Œneus, chief of Calydon, and his wife Althæa.

415. What is the story of his infancy?

It is said that as the child lay sleeping in his cradle, the Mœræ stood suddenly before his mother, and pointing to a log of wood burning on the hearth, told her that as soon as the brand had burnt itself out, Meleagros would die. Althæa, on hearing this, snatched the brand from the fire, and quenching it in water, hid it away in a secret place.[1]

416. How did the child grow up?

Strong, brave, and beautiful, like Œdipus, Perseus, Bellerophon, and the other great heroes. Like them, he achieved great exploits, and especially he took part in the expedition of the Argonauts to recover the golden fleece from Colchis, and in the great Calydonian hunt.

417. Why was this hunt undertaken?

To destroy a monstrous boar which Artemis

---

[1] Tales of Ancient Greece. "Althæa and the Burning Brand."

had sent to punish Œneus, who had neglected to give her her portion of a sacrifice.

418. Who else took part in this boar hunt?

Many of the heroes who shared in the Argonautic expedition; but the foremost of all was Atalantê, the daughter of Schœneus, a chieftain of Arcadia. This beautiful maiden first pierced the boar, which was afterward slain by Meleagros.

419. How were the spoils divided?

Meleagros wished to have the head, and the Curêtes of Pleuron, who had aided the Calydonians in the chase, were not content to have the hide only. Thus a strife arose, in which Meleagros slew the chief of the Curêtes, who was also a brother of Althæa. This was followed by a war between the people of Pleuron and Calydon, in which, after a little while, Meleagros refused to take part, because Althæa, in her grief for the loss of her brother, laid her curse upon her son.

420. What was the consequence of his inaction?

The men of Calydon lost ground and were utterly dismayed, until his wife Cleopatra induced him to go forth. As soon as he appeared the enemies were routed. But the men of Calydon would give him no prize, and Meleagros again withdrew to his secret chambers.

421. Did he come forth again to help his countrymen?

No; Althæa, made yet more angry by his sullenness, brought out the brand and flung it on the fire. As the wood burnt away, the strength of Meleagros decayed, and as the last spark flickered out, he died. The deaths of Althæa and Cleopatra followed soon after that of the great hero.

422. What is the life of Meleagros?

It is the life of the sun, which is bound up with the torch of day; when this torch burns out he dies.

423. In what respect does this story resemble any others?

Meleagros is a counterpart of Perseus, Phœbus, Kephalos and others in his beauty and strength and in his kindly dealings; in the shortness of his life, and his fits of action and inaction, he is throughout like Achilles and Paris.

424. What is this inaction?

It is the veiling of the sun behind the clouds, from which he comes forth either to win the victory like Achilles and Odysseus, or to die like Meleagros and Heracles.

425. What is Atalanta?

A being who may be compared to Daphne and to Artemis, with whose unerring spear she is armed.

426. Why is she described as coming from Arcadia?

Because, like Delos, Lycia, Phœnicia, and other names, Arcadia is a word which originally denoted brightness or splendor.

427. Why should Althæa, after having plucked the brand from the fire, cast it in again?

Because it had been said that, as the sun was the child of the night (Leto, Leda, or Althæa,) so was he also slain by the darkness when his course was done.

428. Who was Phaethon?

A son of Helios and Clymene.[1]

429. What is Helios?

This word has the same origin as the Latin *sol*, and is a name for the sun—Helios standing to Phœbus in the relation of Nereus to Poseidon.

430. How is Helios represented?

As living in a palace of gold, daily driving his chariot drawn by gleaming horses across the heaven, and as having rich herds of cattle.

431. What are these cattle?

They are the bright clouds which Hermes drives across the sky; but in later times, when the meaning of the names was in part forgotten, they were supposed to be cows which were fed in the island of Thrinakia; but even here the real meaning of the story is clear, for they are driven out daily to their pastures by Phaethusa and Lampetie, the *bright* and *glistening* daughters of Neaira, the early morning.

432. What is told about these herds in the Odyssey?

[1] Tales of Ancient Greece. "Phaethon."

It is said that some of the companions of Odysseus killed and ate some of them, and that for this Helios brought about their death.

433. Does the reverence with which the Homeric poet speaks of them show that his countrymen were addicted to beast-worship?

No. It shows only that when the herds of the sun were placed on the earth, they would naturally be regarded as things on which no profaning touch should be laid.

434. What are the horses of Helios?

In the earliest Hindu poems, these are the Harits, who in Greece were changed into beautiful women called Charites, the Latin *Graces*.

435. What is the story of Phaethon?

In an evil hour he is said to have asked his father to let him drive his chariot for a single day. Helios, much against his will, suffered him to take the reins. After rising for a little while into the heaven, the horses, becoming conscious of their driver's weakness, plunged down toward the earth; and the ground, with all its fruits, and streams, and rivers, was parched and dried up. Zeus, seeing that, unless his course was stayed, all living things must soon die, smote Phaethon with his thunderbolts, and the daughters of Hesperus built his tomb on the seashore where he fell.

436. What is the meaning of the name Phaethon?

It means the *bright* or *shining* one, and answers to Phaethusa, as Telephos answers to Telephassa.

437. What is the character of Phaethon?

He possesses some portion of his father's brightness without his power.

438. In this respect does he resemble any other heroes?

Yes; he is the counterpart of Patroclos, who in the Iliad is described as being clothed with the armor of Achilles, and placed in his chariot, which is also drawn by immortal horses, named Xanthos and Balios (the *golden* and *speckled*). Patroclos, like Phaethon, receives directions which he neglects to obey, and like Phaethon, he is slain. In the Odyssey, Telemachus is to Odysseus what Patroclos in the Iliad is to Achilles, and what Phaethon is to Helios.

439. What was the origin of this story?

It grew up from phrases which spoke of drought as caused by the chariot of Helios when driven by some one who knew not how to guide his horses; and the smiting of Phaethon by the bolts of Zeus is the ending of the time of drought by a sudden storm of thunder.

ASKLEPIOS (ÆSCULAPIUS).

440. Who was Asklepios?

In Homer, he is apparently a son or descendant of Paiëon (the healer); but in the commonly received story, he was the son of Apollo and the nymph Coronis, a daughter of Phlegyas, who dwelt on the shores of the lake Bœbêis.

441. What is the legend of his birth?

It is said that before the birth of her child, Apollo left her, having first besought her to continue faithful to him. But when he was gone, a beautiful stranger named Ischys came from Arcadia and won her love. The tidings were brought to Apollo, whose sister Artemis smote Coronis with her unerring spear. But Phœbus saved the babe Asklepios, and gave him into the charge of the centaur Cheiron, who made him wise in the art of healing and in the secret virtues of all herbs.[1]

442. What is the sequel of the tale?

Asklepios gained a world-wide fame and love, as a healer of pain and sickness. But his

[1] Tales of Ancient Greece. "Asklepios."

power of raising the dead roused the wrath of Hades, who complained to Zeus that his kingdom would soon be unpeopled, if Asklepios went on restoring them to the upper world. So Zeus smote Asklepios with his thunderbolt, and this so provoked the anger of Apollo, that he slew the giant Cyclopes. For this offence Zeus banished him to the Stygian land; but on the prayer of his mother Leto the punishment was changed to a year of service in the house of Admetus, who ruled in Pheræ.

443. Is the story of Asklepios told in any other way?

According to some versions, Coronis herself exposed her child, soon after his birth, on a hillside; thus repeating the tale of Paris, Telephus, Œdipus, and other heroes. The child was fed by a goat, as Cyrus was nourished by a dog and Romulus by a wolf. He was found by a shepherd, who was guided to the spot by the blaze of light which surrounded the child. Asklepios was hence called Æglaêr (the shiner), a mere name for the sun.

444. What is Coronis?

A being who in her life and death closely resembles Procris. Like the latter, she is charmed by a stranger who comes with all the beauty of

Phœbus from the Arcadian (or *bright*) land, as Apollo comes from Delos; and like her she is slain by the spear of Artemis.

445. What is the punishment of Apollo?

It is another form of the idea which represents Heracles and Poseidon as toiling in the service of beings weaker than themselves.

446. Whence came the notion of the healing powers of Asklepios.

It is found, in germ, in many legends. The sun was regarded naturally as the restorer of all vegetable life after the long sleep of winter, and as such, his power was extended to the relief of human ailments, and finally to the restoration of the dead to life.

447. Was this god widely worshipped?

Yes. Few deities were more generally honored. His most celebrated temple in Greece was at Epidaurus.

ADMETUS.

448. What is the story of Admetus?

This chief of Pheræ was the happy husband of Alkêstis (Alcestis). But on the day of his marriage he had made Artemis angry by neglecting her in a sacrifice. The goddess, however, promised that when the hour of his death came, he should escape his doom, if his father, mother, or wife would die for him. Alkêstis agreed to do so, and was taken away to Hades; but Heracles found Thanatos (death) on his road to the unseen land, and after a long struggle, rescued her, and brought her back to her home.[1]

449. Does this story throw light on that of Asklepios?

It exhibits Heracles as bringing back the dead after a forcible struggle with Thanatos or Death. But that idea of the wisdom of Phœbus Apollo, which is seen in the legend of Hermes, would naturally suggest the notion that he or his son could restore the sick to health, or recall the dead to life, without any such violent contests.

[1] Thebes and Argos, p. 190.

LYCAON.

450. Who was Lycaon?

He is called a son of Pelasgus, and is said to have built Lycosûra in Arcadïa.

451. What story is told about him?

It is said that when Zeus came to visit Lycaon, he and his twenty or fifty sons set before him a meal of human flesh, and that Zeus, in his anger at this offence, turned them all into wolves.[1]

452. How is this strange tale to be accounted for?

It arose simply from the attempt to explain a name, the true meaning of which had been forgotten.

453. What is the meaning of Lycaon?

Like Delos, Ortygia, Phœnicia, and Lycia, it denoted brightness or splendor. Hence he is placed in Arcadia, which also means the bright land.

454. Whence then came the notion of wolves?

The Greek word Lucos, a wolf, is the same in sound with *Leucos* (white or glistening), whence

---

[1] "Deucalion," Thebes and Argos, p. 191.

came the names Lykios and Lykegenes for Phœbus, and Lucna, Luna, for the moon.

455. Are there other instances of similar changes?

They are very common. Thus Callisto (the fairest) is a daughter of Arcas, the bright one; but the root from which Arcas comes is the same as the root of the word Arctos, a bear; and hence the story went that Callisto, rousing the anger of Artemis, was turned into a bear.

456. Can you mention any other instance?

The constellation now known as Arctus and Arcturus received its name from the root which meant to shine; but for the same reason which changed Callisto into a bear, the notion rose that these stars also were inhabited by bears, and thus came the names of the Great and Little Bear.

457. Was the name changed in India in the same way as in Greece?

Not in the same way, but in exactly the same spirit. The root *ark* there entered into the word *Rishi*, which means a wise man; and hence the seven *arkshas*, or shiners, were changed into the abode of the seven Rishis, or Sages. So again, the word *star* means a *strewer* of light, and is the same as the Hindu word *târâ*; but this word was confused with another like it, which meant a wagon-ox, and hence the constellation came to be also called Charles's Wain or wagon. In the same way Phœbus and Heracles were said to fight with poisoned weapons, because the same sound was used to express the notions of *arrow* and *poison*.

DEUCALION.

458. What is the story of Deucalion?

It is said that in the days of Deucalion, chief of Phthia, and son of Prometheus and Clymene, Zeus resolved to punish the wickedness of men, which had reached its height in the iniquity of Lycaon and his sons. He therefore sent a flood upon the earth, and as the waters rose, Deucalion bade his wife Pyrrha make ready the ark which he had built at the warning of his father Prometheus. Then getting into it, he and his wife were borne for eight days on the waters, and on the ninth the ark rested on the heights of Parnassus. There, having left the ark, they offered sacrifice to Zeus, who sent Hermes to grant any prayer that Deucalion might offer. Deucalion prayed for the restoration of the human race, and Hermes said that he and his wife should cover their faces with their mantles, and cast the bones of their mother behind them as they went on their way. The wisdom which came to him from his father Prometheus, taught him that his mother was the earth, and that they were to cast the stones behind them as they went down from Parnassus. The stones thus thrown became men and women, who at once begin the life of hard toil which ever since that day has been the lot of man.[1]

459. When is this flood said to have taken place?

By some it was assigned to the reign of Ogyges, a mythical king of Athens; but there are many variations in the tale. Some said that all men then perished; others held that the men of Delphi escaped. So in the Babylonish story of Xisuthrus, the flood spares all the pious. In some versions of the Indian tale, Manu enters into the ark with the seven sages or Rishis, who remain with him till it is landed on the peak called Naubandhana, from the binding of the ship.

460. Can the names in this legend be explained?

The name Deucalion is connected with that of Polydeukes (or Pollux), the *brilliant* son of Leda (another form of Leto). His wife Pyrrha, the *red* (perhaps as denoting the red earth), belongs to the same class with Iole, Iocaste, Iamos, the *violet-colored*, and Phoenix, the *purple*.

461. Is the story of Deucalion connected with any other tales?

---

[1] Thebes and Argos, p. 196.

' Yes, with very many. The legend of Prometheus is bound up with that of Io and Heracles, Epimetheus, Pandora, Athena, and others. Deucalion, again, is the father of Minos, the Indian Manu (the *thinker*, or *man*); and Minos is father of Ariadne, whom Theseus led to Naxos after slaying the Minotaur. Minos is further connected with the Argive tale of Nisos and Skylla (Scylla).

462. Are any other children of Deucalion mentioned?

He is also called the father of Hellen (from whom the Hellenes or Greeks are said to have sprung), and of Protogeneia, the early morning, the *first-born* of the sun.

463. Is the story carried on in the same spirit?

Yes. Protogeneia, the dawn, becomes the mother of Aethlios, the toiling and striving sun, who, like Heracles and Achilles, labors for others, not for himself: and Aethlios is the father of Endymion the fair, who sinks to sleep in the Latmian cave, as the sun plunges into the western sea.

464. Is the story of Deucalion retained in the traditions of any other people?

The Macusi-Indians of South America relate, it is said, that the last man who survived the flood repeopled the earth by changing stones into men. According to the Tamanaks of Orinoko, it was a pair of human beings who cast behind them the fruit of a certain palm, and out of the kernels sprang men and women.

IO.

465. Who was Io?

Io is called a daughter of Inachus, king of Argos. She is said to have been loved by Zeus, who changed her into a heifer to protect her against the jealousy of Hera. Hera, however, gained possession of Io by prevailing on Zeus to grant her that which she might desire, and gave her in charge to Argos Panoptes, the all-seeing.

466. How was she rescued from Argos?

None were able to surprise Argos, whose eyes were never closed, until Hermes, the messenger of Zeus, approached with his soft and lulling music, and then slew him when at last he slept. In revenge for this, Hera sent a gadfly, which stung the heifer Io, and drove her in agony from land to land, through Thebes and Thrace, until she reached the desolate heights of Caucasus, where the Titan Prometheus hung chained to the rock, while a vulture gnawed his liver.[1]

467. Who was Prometheus?

[1] Tales of Ancient Greece. "Io and Prometheus."

The mighty being who aided Zeus in his war against Cronos, and who taught men how to build houses and obey law, and brought them down fire from heaven. This act roused the anger of Zeus, who, forgetting all gratitude, had Prometheus chained to the icebound rocks of Caucasus.

468. What did Io learn from Prometheus?

He told her that her wanderings were little more than begun; that she must go from thence through the land of the Amazons, across the strait, which from her should be called Bosporus, into Asia, and thence into the Æthopian land, where she should become the mother of Epaphus, from whom should hereafter spring Heracles, and that by Heracles Prometheus should be delivered from his terrible punishment.

469. Were these predictions fulfilled?

Yes, according to the generally received tale.

470. How did the Greeks regard the legend?

As pointing to a connection between Greece and Egypt; Io being identified with Isis, and Epaphus with the calf-god Apis. But, as in the case of the Sphinx, this notion is the fancy of a later age.

471. What name was given to Hermes, as being the slayer of Argos?

He was called Argeiphontes, just as Hipponoös was called Bellerophon or Bellerophontes, because he smote Belleros.

472. Who are the Amazons?

They were supposed to be a tribe of warlike women, who lived on the banks of the Thermodon, suffering no man to dwell among them. They were said to have been so called from the practice of cutting off the right breast, to give them greater freedom in using the bow.

473. Is this explanation correct?

No. The story grew up because the meaning of the word had been forgotten, as in the case of Lycaon, Arctos, Œdipus, and many others.

474. Is the name of Prometheus found in any other traditions?

It is the Pramantha of the Hindus, who use it to denote the churn for churning fire with pieces of dried sticks.

475. What does Herodotus tell us about Io?

His story is that when a Phœnician merchant-ship chanced to come to Argos, she went on board to make choice of things to be purchased; that the captain of the vessel carried her away, either with or against her will, and that this offence led the Greeks to make reprisals by carrying off Medea from Colchis.

476. What resemblance has this to the other tale?

None whatever; the only point in common between them is that Io is carried into Asia.

477. Is Herodotus, then, speaking of the same Io?

Clearly he is; for he calls her the daughter of Inachus.

478. How is his version of the story to be accounted for?

When the marvellous incidents of the old legends came to be thought incredible, Herodotus and other writers fancied that they could mend matters by putting aside all that was marvellous in each story, and then regarding it as still the same story. Thus, according to him, Io was not changed into a heifer, and never talked with Prometheus. In the same way the historian Thucydides makes a very plausible history of the Trojan war, by leaving out all that is said about Hector, and Helen, and Achilles, and all the other actors in the tale.

479. Is this method trustworthy?

It is neither more nor less trustworthy than the story of Jack the Giant-killer would be, if we were to say that he never climbed up to the sky on a bean-stalk, and that he never killed any giants, because there were no giants to kill.

EPIMETHEUS.

480. Who was Epimetheus?

The brother of Prometheus.

481. What is the meaning of the name?

Epimetheus is one who takes thought after an event, while Prometheus is one who considers the matter well beforehand.

482. What is the story told about Epimetheus?

It is said that, before it was settled what part out of each victim sacrificed should be given to the gods, Prometheus slew an ox, and placing the entrails and flesh under the skin, put the bones under the fat, and told Zeus to take which he pleased. Zeus placed his hand on the fat, and was wroth at finding that his portion was simply fat and bone. Hence, when Prometheus was gone, he determined to punish Epimetheus, who had been warned by his brother to receive no gift from the gods.[1]

483. Was Epimetheus tempted to neglect this warning?

Yes. Zeus commanded Hephæstus to take earth, and fashion it into the shape of a woman.

---

[1] Tales of Ancient Greece. "Epimetheus and Pandora."

This moulded image Athena clad in a beautiful robe, while Hermes gave her the power of words, and a greedy mind, to cheat and deceive mankind. Zeus then led Pandora (for so she was named) to Epimetheus, who received her into his house. There Pandora saw a great cask on the threshold and lifted the lid; and from it came strife and war, plague and sickness, and all other evils. In her fright she let down the lid upon the cask, and left Hope shut up within it, so that men had nothing to make their wretchedness more tolerable.

484. Is this story of Pandora's box understood in any other way?

Some think that Hope was shut up in the cask out of mercy to men, and not to heighten their misery. But this is not the meaning of the story in Hesiod, for Pandora does not bring the cask with her: she finds it in the house of Epimetheus, and the diseases and evils can do no hurt until they are let loose. Hence the shutting up of Hope only makes matters worse instead of better.

485. Is the story of Prometheus inconsistent with any other legend?

Yes; it wholly contradicts the Hesiodic story of the Five Ages—the Golden, the Silver, the

Brazen, the Heroic, and the Iron. This tradition supposes that men lived at first free from want or pain, or sickness or misery of any kind, until Pandora came and let all evils loose. But the story of Prometheus supposes that the earliest state of man was one of utter wretchedness, and that their life was that of brute beasts, until he gave them houses and fire, and made them live in decency and order. This notion is also found in the story of Phoroneus.

DÆDALUS.

486. What is the story of Dædalus?

The tales recounted of him are by no means consistent. The commonly received version calls him a son or descendant of Erechtheus, the father of Procris, and says that he was banished for murdering Calos, because he surpassed him in skill of workmanship. Dædalus then went to Crete, where he made the wooden cow for Pasiphae, and also constructed the labyrinth for the Minotaur. For doing this he was shut up by Minos; and as no ships were left on the coast, Dædalus fashioned a pair of wings for himself, and another for his son Icarus, and fastened them on with wax. Dædalus thus made his escape to Sicily; but Icarus mounted too near the sun, and, melting the wax of his wings, fell into the Icarian sea and was drowned. Nothing more is recorded of Dædalus, except that he executed many great works of art in the west.

487. What is the meaning of his name?

It means simply the cunning or wise workman; and the same idea is found in the epithet Polymetis, constantly applied to Odysseus, who also made a beautiful bridal-chamber for his wife Penelope. The wisdom of Dædalus is, in fact, only another form of the wisdom of Phœbus and Œdipus.

488. What is Icarus?

A feeble reflection of his father, as Phaethon is of Helios, and Telemachus of Odysseus.

NIOBE.

389. Who was Niobe?

Almost every incident in the story of Niobe is told in many ways. Thus by some she is called the mother of Phoroneus, and the wife of Inachus; but the more popular version makes her a daughter of Tantalus, and the wife of Amphion, king of Thebes. Contrasting the number of her six sons and daughters with the two children of whom alone Leto was the mother, she roused the wrath of Leto, who bade Phœbus and Artemis to avenge the affront. Accordingly they slew all the children of Niobe with the arrows which never miss their mark, and Niobe, going to the mountain of Sipylus, there wept herself into stone.[1]

400. What is the meaning of this story?

The rivalry between Niobe and Leto is reproduced in that between Medusa and Athena; and the many children of Niobe are the many children of the mist—in other words, the clouds; which, although as beautiful as Phœbus and Artemis, are dried up by the burning rays of the sun, while Niobe herself dissolves in a rain of tears, which turns into hard ice on the mountain summit.

[1] "Niobe and Leto." Tales of Ancient Greece.

TANTALUS.

491. What is the story of Tantalus?

He is said to have been a king of Lydia, who had a palace blazing with gold beneath Mount Sipylus, where Niobe wept herself to stone. He was as widely known for his wisdom and power as his wife, Euryanassa, was for her beauty. Indeed, Tantalus was admitted to share the secret counsels of Zeus, and thus gained a knowledge beyond the reach of mortals. But in course of time he stole some of the food and drink of the gods, and gave them to his people; and he also refused to give up the dog Pandareos, who had guarded Zeus in the cave of Dictê. Finally, when Zeus and all the gods came down to feast in his banquet hall, he cut up his own child Pelops, and placed his roasted limbs before them as a repast. Pelops was restored to life by Zeus, who doomed Tantalus to gaze on beautiful fruits which he might not touch, and on clear waters which he might not taste. If he bowed his head to drink, the waters fled away: if he put forth his hand to pluck the fruit, the branches which bore them vanished, and a huge rock appearing above his head threatened to crush him to powder.[1]

492. Can this story be explained?

It is one of the most transparent of Greek legends. The palace of Tantalus is the golden house of Helios, from which Phaeton goes forth on his luckless journey. His wisdom is the wisdom of Phœbus, Œdipus, and Odysseus. His frequent converse with Zeus represents the daily visits of Helios to the heights of heaven. His theft of nectar and ambrosia answers to the theft of fire by Prometheus, and the wealth which he bestows on the people is the wealth which the warmth of the sun draws forth from the earth. But as the sun, when his heat becomes too great, burns up these fruits, so, when such drought came, men said, "Tantalus is slaying and roasting his own child." The restoration of Pelops to life is the action of that mighty power which restores freshness to the earth after drought, and which is wielded by Asklepios and Medea. The sentence passed on Tantalus agrees closely with the same idea. His stooping to drink the water and eat the

[1] Tales of Ancient Greece.

fruits which surround him points to the drying up of streams and the withering of herbage by the fierce rays of the sun. The rock which threatens to crush him is the dark stormcloud which broods like the Sphinx over the earth, or frowns like Polyphemus on Odysseus. And as the earth is the more scorched in proportion as the sun may be said to stoop nearer down to it, the expression "to be tantalized" is applied to all disappointments when the prize sought seems within our grasp.

493. Who is Euryanassa?

The broad-ruling day—a name corresponding to Eurymedusa, Euryphassa, Europa, all names for the morning or the day.

IXION.

494. Who was Ixion?

By some he is called a son of Phlegyas (the flaming one), and he is said to have married Dia, the daughter of Hesioneus, to whom he promised rich gifts, which, after the marriage, he refused to send.

495. How did Hesioneus bear this refusal?

He stole the undying horses which bore the gleaming chariot of Ixion, who told Hesioneus to come and take the gifts if he wished to have them. Hesioneus went accordingly, and when he insisted on seeing the treasure-house where the gifts were stored, Ixion opened the door, and Hesioneus fell into a pit full of fire.[1]

496. What followed this murder?

A time of drought and wretchedness until Zeus purified Ixion from his guilt.

497. How did Ixion requite this kindness?

By offering his love to Hera, the queen of heaven.

498. How did Zeus meet this new danger?

[1] Tales of Ancient Greece. "Ixion."

He made a cloud assume the likeness of Hera, and thus deceived Ixion, who became the father of the Kentaurs (Centaurs); and to punish Ixion still further, he bound him to a four-spoked wheel which bears him round forever and ever.

499. What is the meaning of this tale?

Like that of Tantalus, it describes some part of the action of the sun in its journey through the sky.

500. What is Dia?

A being who represents the fair Dawn, and who answers to Dahana, Daphne, Iole, Iocaste, and Eurydike. As Heracles forsakes Iole, and Sigurd leaves Brynhild, as Œdipus and Orpheus are parted from Iocaste and Eurydike, and as Theseus deserts Ariadne, so Ixion leaves Dia, and is smitten with the charms of Hera.

501. What is Hesioneus?

The darkness from which Dia, the dawn, springs.

502. What is the treasure-house of Ixion?

It is the palace of Helios and Tantalus, the abyss of splendor in which the Night is consumed.

503. Why is Ixion made to love the lady Hera?

Because the sun, as it rises in the heaven,

may be said to woo the blue sky, which was specially the abode of Hera and Zeus.

504. What is the sojourn of Ixion in the house of Zeus?

It is the long pause which the sun seems to make in the highest heaven at noon-tide.

505. What is the phantom which cheats Ixion?

The beautiful cloud which reposes on the deep blue sky; and the Kentaurs, the Indian Gandharvas, are its children—the vapors which expand from the little cloud during the rainy time in eastern lands.

506. What is the four-spoked wheel of Ixion?

. It is the fiery cross which is seen in the sky by those who look on the sun at noonday.

507. Can the name Ixion be explained?

It has been identified by some with the Sanskrit word Akshanah, denoting one who is bound to a wheel; the word Ixion being thus regarded as akin to the Greek axôn, the Latin axis, and the English axle.

508. Is the germ of the story of Ixion found in these old poems?

It is said that Dyaus (the sky) struggled hard to snatch the wheel of the sun from the grasp of Night. From such phrases sprung the notion of the dark Gorgons chasing Perseus as he hastens to the Hyperborean gardens.

BELLEROPHON, OR BELLEROPHONTES.

509. What is the meaning of the word Bellerophon?

It means the slayer of Belleros, as Hermes is called Argeiphontes, because he slew Argus; and the name was given to Hipponoös, the son of Glaucos (the bright or shining one).

510. Who was the father of Glaucos?

Sisyphus, the crafty, whose punishment in Tartarus is to roll to the top of a hill a stone which immediately rolls down again, just as the sun is forced to descend as soon as he has reached the highest point in his course through the heaven.

511. What is the story of Bellerophon?

After slaying Belleros, he fled to the court of Prœtus, whose wife, Anteia, fell in love with Bellerophon, who shut his ears to her persuasions. Anteia then accused him to Prœtus of an attempt to corrupt her, and Prœtus sent him to Iobates, king of Lydia, with letters charging him to put the bearer to death. This Iobates would not do, but he imposed on Bellerophon some hard tasks. Bellerophon accordingly slew the Chimæra, which had the head of a lion, the body of a goat, and the tail of a dragon.

512. How did he accomplish this?

By the aid of the winged horse Pegasus, which he had caught while drinking at the fountain of Pirênê.

513. What were his next exploits?

He conquered the Solymi and Amazons, and then he married the daughter of Iobates, after which he tried to rise to heaven on Pegasus, but Zeus sent a gadfly which stung the horse and made him throw his rider. Bellerophon was not killed, but his strength was broken, and after wandering for some time alone on the Aleian plain, he died.[1]

514. Does this story resemble any others?

The tasks imposed on Bellerophon answer exactly to the labors of Heracles, Perseus, Theseus, and other heroes. His rejection of the love of Anteia is the desertion of Brynhild by Sigurd, or of Œnone by Paris. So after slaying the Chimæra, he wins his bride, as Œdipus wins Iocastê after conquering the Sphinx, and Perseus is wedded to Andromeda after killing the Libyan dragon. His attempt to fly to heaven

[1] Tales of Ancient Greece. "Bellerophon."

is the attempt of Phaethon to drive the chariot of Helios, and of Ixion to gain possession of Hera. The gadfly which stings Pegasus reappears in the story of Io. The fall of Bellerophon is the rapid descent of the sun toward evening, and the Aleian plain is that broad expanse of sombre light through which the sun is sometimes seen to travel sullenly and alone to his setting.

SKYLLA (SCYLLA).

515. Who was Skylla?

She is called a daughter of Nisos, king of Megara.

516. What story is told about her?

She is said to have fallen in love with Minos when he came to take vengeance for the death of his son Androgeos. When Minos failed in all his attempts to take the city, Skylla shore off the purple locks of hair on the head of Nisus, on which the safety of the city depended. As soon as Minos had the locks in his possession, Megara was taken; but far from returning her love, Minos, according to one story, drowned her in the sea: in another, she was turned into a fish, which Nisos changed into an eagle, instantly pursued.

517. Who was Minos?

A son of Europa and Zeus, who is said to have been king of Crete, and who, after his death, became, with Rhadamanthus and Æacus, one of the judges of the dead. He is the same as the Indian Manu, the son of Brahma.

518. What is the magic lock of Nisus?

It represents the golden rays of Phœbus, the sun-god, who is called Akersekomes, or the being whose head is not touched with a razor.

IAMOS.

519. Who was Iamos?

A son of Phœbus and Evadne, born on the banks of the Alpheius. On his birth Evadne, fearing the wrath of her father Æpytus, chief of Phæsana, fled away, and Phœbus sent two serpents who guarded the child and fed him with honey. Æpytus, after a long search, found the babe lying on a bed of violets; and the child soon showed himself possessed of a marvellous wisdom, for Phœbus, touching his ears, made him understand the voices of birds, and underneath the waters of Alpheius Iamos had gained a knowledge of things hidden from the minds of men. His children, the Iamidæ, were the famous seers or prophets of Olympia.[1]

520. What likeness has this legend to others?

The exposure of Iamos is the same as that of Œdipus, Perseus, Telephus, and other heroes. The snakes are here, as elsewhere, the serpents of night; but as in the old phrases the night was described sometimes as dark and gloomy, sometimes as lovely and gentle, so here the

---
[1] Tales of Ancient Greece. "Iamos."

snakes which seek to sting Heracles are represented as nursing Iamos.

521. What is the meaning of the name Iamos?

The meaning has been rightly preserved in the story. Like Iole, Iocaste, and others, it denotes the violet tints of the morning.

522. What is the wisdom of Iamos?

It is the wisdom of Phœbus, which he imparted to his son Asklepios and in part to Hermes, and which is shared also by Medea.

AMPHIARAOS.

523. Who was Amphiaraos?

A descendant of the wise seer Melampus, whose ears, being cleansed by serpents, were enabled to catch the utterances of birds.

524. Was this power granted to any other?

Yes; to Iamos.

525. What exploits are attributed to Amphiaraos?

He took part in the Calydonian boar-hunt and the Argonautic expedition, and finally in the war at Thebes waged by Polyneikes against his brother Eteocles. With this strife Amphiaraos wished to have nothing to do; but his wife Eriphyle, bribed by the necklace which Cadmus gave to Harmonia, betrayed her husband's lurking-place. When, in the fight which followed the death of the sons of Œdipus, Amphiaraos found himself hard pressed, he prayed to Zeus, who caused the earth to open and swallow up his chariot.

526. What was the recompense of Eriphyle?

She was killed by her son Alcmæon, who, after long wanderings, found rest on the islands at the mouth of the river Achelöus.

527. Was this the end of Alcmæon's history?

No. He led the Epigoni (the sons of the chiefs who had fought in the former war) to that attack upon Thebes which ended with the destruction of the city.

BRIAREOS (BRIAREUS).

528. Who was Briareos?

The hundred-handed son of Ouranos and Gaia, otherwise called Ægæon. When Hera, Poseidon, and Athena were going to bind Zeus, Thetis warned him of his danger, and Zeus, summoning Briareos to his side, so frightened the conspirators that they gave up their attempt.

ARETHUSA.

529. Who was Arethusa?

One of the Nereids, or daughters of Nereus, who stands to Poseidon in the relation of Helios to Phœbus.

530. What story is told of her?

The hunter Alpheius is said to have pursued her, as Apollo pursued Daphne; and like Daphne, Arethusa, to escape from him, threw herself into the stream, and the nymphs carried her to the Ortygian shore. Thither Alpheius followed her; and, driven to despair, Arethusa plunged into the fountain which bears her name. Alpheius, unable to bear her loss, also plunged into the waters, beneath which he won the love which she had refused him during life.[1]

531. What is the meaning of this tale?

It is the parting of Heracles and Iole, who meets him again when his toils are ended. The shore on which Arethusa and Alpheius meet is the land of the morning and evening twilight.

[1] Tales of Ancient Greece. "Arethusa."

TYRO.

532. Who was Tyro?

The bride of the river Enipeus, and mother of Pelias and Neleus.

533. What is the legend of Tyro?

When her children were born, her father Salmoneus, who had married the iron-hearted Sidero, ordered them to be killed; they were, accordingly, exposed on the river's banks, where they were rescued by a herdsman. When they were grown up, they put Sidero to death, and delivered Tyro from the dungeon in which she had been imprisoned by Salmoneus because she refused to become the wife of Cretheus.[1]

534. What other story does this tale resemble?

It is only another form of the legend of Danae. Pelias and Neleus are exposed like Perseus, and rescued in the same way with Cyrus, Romulus, and Remus. As Danae refuses to marry Polydectes, so Tyro rejects the hand of Cretheus; and as Perseus brings Danae back to Argos, after avenging her of her persecutors, so Pelias and Neleus set free their mother after they have slain her tormentor, Sidero.

[1] Tales of Ancient Greece. "Tyro."

NARCISSUS.

535. What is the story of Narcissus?

This son of the river Kephisos (Cephisus) was loved by the nymph Echo, who, failing to win his love in return, died of grief. As a punishment, Nemesis made Narcissus fall in love with his own image reflected in water, and the youth, in his turn, pined away from unsatisfied longing. On the spot where he died, the flower sprang up which is called by his name. Later versions said that he was turned into a narcissus, as they also said that Daphne was changed into a laurel.[1]

536. What is the love of Echo for Narcissus?

It is only another version of the love of Selene for Endymion (the sun just plunging into the sea); and as Endymion sleeps in Latmos (the land of forgetfulness), so the name Narcissus denotes the numbness or deadness of profound sleep, and thus expresses precisely the same idea which marks the legend of Endymion.

[1] Tales of Ancient Greece. "Narkissos."

THE ARGONAUTS.

537. What was the Argonautic expedition?

An expedition of many Achaian chieftains to recover the golden fleece.

538. What was the golden fleece?

It belonged to the golden ram of Phrixus.

539. What is the story of Phrixus?

He is called the son of Athamas and Nephele. On the death of Nephele, Athamas married Ino, and Phrixus with his sister Hellê lived in great unhappiness until a ram with a golden fleece carried them away. As it soared through the air, Hellê fell off its back, and was drowned in the Hellespont, which bears her name. Phrixus was carried onward to the palace of Æetes king of Colchis, and there he sacrificed to Zeus, the guardian of fugitives, the ram who had borne him thither. The golden fleece was hung up in the house of Æetes, until the Achaian chieftains, urged on by Athamas, came to claim it.[1]

540. How was the expedition planned?

There are many versions to the story; but

---

[1] Tales of Ancient Greece. "Phrixos and Hellc."

the one most commonly received states that Pelias, a nephew of Jason, had received a warning to be on his guard against a man with only one shoe, and that when Jason appeared at a sacrifice, having lost one of his sandals in a stream, Pelias bade him go and fetch the golden fleece from Colchis. Jason, accordingly, gathered all the great chieftains round about, and sailed away in the ship Argo, which was endowed with the power of speech. Among those who went with him were Heracles, Meleagros, Amphiaraos, Admetus, and other heroes. Sailing eastward they passed through the dangerous rocks called Symplegades, which opened and were again closed continually with such quickness that a bird had scarcely time to fly through. Tiphys steered the vessel safely through these rocks, which thenceforth became fixed. Having passed through the land of the Amazons, they at last reached Colchis, where Jason demanded the fleece from Æetes, who refused to give it up until Jason had ploughed the land with the fire-breathing bulls and sown it with the dragon's teeth. This he was enabled to do by the aid of Medea, who anointed his body with an ointment which protected him against the fiery breath of the bulls, and told him to cast a stone among the armed men who would spring up from the dragon's teeth.

541. What was the result?

As soon as Jason threw the stone, the men began to fight with each other, until all were slain. Then Medea lulled to sleep the dragon which guarded the fleece, and Jason, slaying the monster, gained possession of the treasure, and hastened away in the ship Argo.

542. What incidents belong to the return voyage?

Æetes pursued the ship in hot haste; and Medea, who had fled with Jason, cut up her brother Apsyrtus, and threw his limbs one by one into the sea. Æetes stopped to pick them up, and the ship thus passed beyond his reach.

543. What happened on Jason's return to Iolcos?

Medea persuaded the daughters of Pelias to cut up the body of their father, and place them in a caldron, saying that she would restore him again to life as in his youth. They obeyed; but Medea, pretending to be looking at the stars to know the right moment for using her spells, allowed his limbs to be consumed, and thus the warning given to Pelias was fulfilled.

544. Did Jason remain at Iolcos?

No. Medea took him in her dragon chariot

to Argos, where Jason was smitten with the beauty of Glaukê, the daughter of Creon.

545. Did Medea bear this patiently?

She seemed to be well pleased, and sent to Glaukê as a bridal gift the beautiful robe which Helios gave her before she left her father's house. No sooner had the maiden put it on than the robe began to burn her flesh, and Creon, who tried to tear it off, died with his child. Medea then vanished from Argos in her dragon chariot.[1]

546. Is anything further recorded of Medea?

She is said to have killed her two children, the sons of Jason.

547. How did this strange and terrible story spring up?

From phrases which described the changes of day and night.

548. How is this shown?

The sun, who is called Helios Hyperion (the climber), was said to go down in the evening into a golden cup or vessel, which carried him across the ocean stream to the abode of black night, where he found his mother, his wife, and his children, and from this cup he rose again in the morning.

[1] Tales of Ancient Greece. "Medeia."

549. How does this bear on the story of the Argonauts?

As in the oldest Indian poems the departure of the sun left men in grief and fear, the idea of a search for their lost friend naturally suggested itself; and all the things which he had cherished with his warmth in the daytime were supposed to seek for him until they found him and brought him back again.

550. What, then, is the ship Argo?

It is a symbol of the earth as a parent, which contains in itself the germs of all living things. Hence it carries all the Achaian chieftains, who return with renewed strength and vigor when their mission is accomplished.

551. Why is it gifted with the power of speech?

As the parent of all things, the earth was regarded as a conscious being, endowed with the power of thought, sight, and language.

552. What is the golden fleece?

The golden garment (or rays) of the sun, which reappears as the robe given by Helios to Medea, and which may either warm or scorch those whom it may touch. It is the same robe which Nessus gives to Deianeira, and which consumes the body of Heracles.

553. What is Medea?

A being who possesses that wisdom which belongs to Phœbus Apollo by his birthright. This wisdom is inherited by Asklepios and Tantalus, as representing the sun, who can see into the hidden secrets of Zeus (the sky). This notion, when applied to Medea as a wise woman, suggested the idea of witchcraft or sorcery.

554. What is the story of the dragon's teeth?

Another version of the turning of stones into men in the legend of Deucalion.

555. Why does Æetes pursue the retreating Argo?

Because the Gorgons chase Perseus, as the darkness may be said to chase the sun who leaves it behind him as he rises in the sky.

556. What are the life-giving powers of Medea?

The same sun which causes deadly drought also recalls all things to life after the slumber of night and the long sleep of winter. Hence Medea, like Tantalus and Lycaon, is able to slay, and, like Asklepios and Heracles, to restore the dead to life.

557. What is the dragon chariot of Medea?

It is the same as the chariot of Indra, Helios, and Achilles. That of Indra is drawn by the Harits (who in western legends became the Graces), that of Helios and Achilles by undying horses. The chariot of Medea is drawn by dragons, because the word *dragon* means one who has keen sight, and the name was naturally applied to the creatures which may be supposed to bear the sun through the heaven.

THE TALE OF TROY.

558. What is the tale of Troy or Ilion?

It consists of that series of legends which together make up the mythical history of Paris, Helen, Achilles, and Odysseus.

559. Is the whole of this tale contained in the Iliad and Odyssey, which are generally called the poems of Homer?

No; but there are expressions and hints scattered throughout the poems which seem to show that the poets were acquainted with many incidents, about which they did not care to speak.

560. How does this tale begin?

With the birth of Paris, whose mother Hecabê (Hecuba) dreamt that her son was a torch which would destroy the land of Ilion.

561. What was the consequence of this dream?

The child was exposed on the heathy sides of mount Ida; but he was rescued by a shepherd, and growing up beautiful, brave, and generous, he was called Alexandros, the helper of men.

562. How was Paris made known to his parents?

His father, Priam, ordered a sacrifice to be offered up for the repose of Paris in Hades, and his servants chose the favorite bull of Paris, who followed them and was conqueror in his own funeral games. Although no one else recognized him, his sister Casandra, to whom Phœbus had given the power of second-sight, under the penalty that her predictions should not be believed, told them who the victor was.

563. Did Paris remain in Troy?

He refused to stay with those who had treated him so cruelly in his infancy, and in the dells of Ida he won Œnônê, the beautiful daughter of the stream Kebrên, as his bride.

564. How long did he remain with Œnônê?

Until he departed for Sparta with Menelaüs.

565. How was this brought about?

At the marriage-feast of Peleus with Thetis, the mother of Achilles, Eris (strife), who had not been invited with the other gods, cast on the table a golden apple, which was to be given to the fairest of all the guests. It was claimed by Hera, Athena, and Aphrodite, and Zeus made Paris the umpire. By him it was given to Aphrodite, who promised him in return Helen, the loveliest of all women, as his wife. Some time after this, there fell on Sparta a sore famine, from which the Delphian oracle said that they could be delivered only by bringing back the bones of the children of Prometheus. For this purpose, Menelaüs, the king, came to Ilion, and returned with Paris, who saw the beautiful Helen at Sparta, and winning her love, carried her away to Troy.

566. How did Menelaüs bear the loss of Helen?

He determined to rescue her from Paris, and he invited Agamemnon, king of Mykenæ, and other great chieftains, to take part in the expedition.

567. Mention the names of some of these chiefs?

Nestor, the wise ruler of Pylos; Ajax the son of Telamon; Ascalaphos and Ialmenos, sons of Ares; Diomedes, son of Tydeus, and Admetus, the husband of Alkêstis. But the greatest of all was Achilles, the son of Peleus and the seanymph Thetis, and Odysseus, the son of Laertes who ruled in Ithaca.

568. How did they go to Troy?

By sea; but the fleet was becalmed in Aulis, and Calchas, the seer, affirming that this was caused by the anger of Artemis for the slaughter of a stag in her sacred grove, declared that she could be appeased only by the sacrifice of Iphigeneia, the daughter of Agamemnon.¹

569. Was the sacrifice made?

Yes, according to the Homeric story; but others said that Artemis herself rescued Iphigeneia, who became a priestess of the goddess: others again said that Artemis and Iphigeneia were the same person.

570. What was the consequence of this deed?

Atê, who takes vengeance for the shedding of innocent blood, brooded over the house of Agamemnon, until she had brought about the death of the king by the hands of his wife Clytæmnestra, and the death of Clytæmnestra by the hands of her son Orestes.

571. What was the prophecy of Calchas, when Iphigeneia was sacrificed?

He said that the Achaians would fight in vain for nine years, but that in the tenth year Ilion would be taken.

572. By whom was Troy defended?

Chiefly by Hector, son of Priam, and brother of Paris, aided by the chiefs of neighboring cities, among whom were Æneas, the son of Anchises and Aphrodite; Pandarus the son of

---

¹ Tales of ancient Greece. "Iphigeneia."

Lycaon, and bearer of the bow of Apollo; and Sarpedon, who, with his friend Glaucus, led the Lycians from the banks of the eddying Xanthos.

573. What is the story of Sarpedon?

Like Achilles, Meleagros, Sigurd, and other heroes, he is doomed to an early death, which Zeus, his father, vainly strives to avert. Fighting bravely, he was smitten by the spear of Patroclos, the friend of Achilles, and the tears of Zeus (the sky) fell in big drops of rain at his untimely fate. Then Phœbus bathed the body of Sarpedon in the pure waters of Simoeis, and Hupnos and Thanatos bore it, at the bidding of Zeus, through the still hours of night, to his home far away in Lycia.[1]

574. What is the meaning of this story?

Sarpedon is a name springing from the same root with Hermes, Helen, Erinys, Saranyu, and *serpent*, and denotes the morning light as it creeps across the sky. Like Phœbus, he is king of Lycia (the bright land, a name belonging to the same class with Delos, Ortygia, Argos, Arcadia, Athens, Phœnicia, and Ethiopia), through which flows Xanthos, the *golden* stream of light. Hence his friend is called Glaucos, the *brilliant*.

[1] Tales of Ancient Greece. "Sarpedon."

The death of Sarpedon, and the carrying of his body home during the night, answer to the nightly voyage of Helios in his golden cup or vessel along the stream of Ocean which flows round the world of men; and the same idea, slightly altered, is found in the voyage of the Argonauts for the golden fleece, or sunlight, which has been stolen away.

575. Is there any other Trojan hero who closely resembles Sarpedon?

Yes. Like him, Memnon, the son of Eos (the morning), whose jealousy causes the death of the beautiful Procris, comes from Æthiopia, the glistening land.[1] Like him, he is doomed to an early death, and when he is smitten by the hand of Achilles, the tears of Eos fall as morning dew from the sky. Then she went and stood before Zeus, and besought him to bring Memnon up from Hades. Zeus granted her prayer, and Memnon accordingly rose with Eos to Olympus, as the sun rises from the dark land of night in the morning.

576. Who was the father of Memnon?

Tithonos, whose couch, as the mythical phrase went, Eos left every morning to bring back daylight to the sons of men. Eos obtained for him

[1] Tales of Ancient Greece. "Memnon."

the boon of immortality, but as she forgot to ask for perpetual youth, Tithonos became decrepit, and was doomed to an everlasting old age.

577. What is the story of Achilles in the Trojan war?

In all its main features it is a counterpart of that of Meleagros, which, with other similar tales, seems to have furnished the foundation for the more finished Homeric legend.

578. What is the subject of the Iliad?

It professes to relate the wrath of Achilles.

579. What was the cause of this wrath?

Achilles loved Briseis, whom Agamemnon, when forced to restore Chryseis to her father, took away from the hero's tent. Enraged at this act, Achilles made a solemn vow that he would no longer take part in the war, and told the chiefs that they would speedily feel his absence from the battle-field.

580. Was this prediction fulfilled?

Not according to the poem, which, as a whole, is now called the Iliad; for it goes on to show, through many books, that the Achaian heroes got on perfectly well without Achilles, and obtained great victories over the Trojans.

581. What are we to conclude from this contradiction?

That the poem called the Iliad consists of two poems which have been strung together, and that the one poem relates the exploits of the Achaian chiefs, and is really the Iliad, while the other describes the wrath of Achilles, and is really the Achillêis.

582. Was the wrath of Achilles appeased?

Not until the Achaians had been brought to great distress, and were compelled to beg humbly for his aid.

583. How did the other chiefs venture near Achilles in his terrible anger?

Odysseus and others went with Phœnix at their head, and Phœnix, who had been the teacher of Achilles in his boyhood, recited to him the story of Meleagros, as an example of the wretched evil which inordinate anger brings with it.

584. Does this appease Achilles?

No; he insists that Agamemnon, who did him the wrong, should make atonement by humble submission, and by the restoration of Briseis.

585. Was this submission made?

Not immediately; and the disasters of the Achaians so troubled Patroclos, the friend of Achilles, that he went to the hero and besought him to let him go forth in his chariot and with his armor to fight the Trojans.

586. Did Achilles grant this prayer?

Yes; but he gave him at the same time strict charge to fight in the plain, and not to drive his chariot against the city.

587. Was this command obeyed?

Not thoroughly; and thus Patroclos, after having slain Sarpedon, was himself overpowered and killed by Hector, who stripped off from his body the glistening armor of Achilles.

588. How did Achilles receive the tidings of his death?

He tore his hair, and rending his clothes, lay down weeping in the dust. That which prayers and entreaties had been unable to obtain, was wrung from him by his overpowering grief and rage. Achilles swore to take vengeance against Hector, and to sacrifice twelve Trojan youths on the funeral pile of his friend.

589. But how could he go to fight without his armor?

At the prayer of Thetis, Hephæstus forged him a new suit, which bore him aloft like a bird upon the wing; and his spear and sword were still in his tent, for these no mortal hands might wield but those of Achilles.

590. What warning did Thetis give to her son, when he swore to take the life of Hector?

She told him that his own death would soon follow that of Hector.

591. What was the answer of Achilles?

He said that he was well content to die the death of Heracles, if only Hector died before him.

592. Was this the only warning received by Achilles?

No. When he mounted his chariot, and bade his immortal steeds bring him back safe from the battle-field, the horse Xanthos bowed his head, and told him that his life was nearly done.

593. What effect had the reappearance of Achilles?

At a glance of his eye and the sound of his voice, the Trojans were filled with fear, and they trembled as the Myrmidons, the followers of Achilles, rushed to the battle like wolves with blood-red jaws greedy for the carnage.[1]

594. What was the issue of the fight?

After fighting bravely, Hector fell, pierced with the unerring lance of Achilles, who trampled on his body, and having tied it to his chariot, dragged it furiously along the ground, until none could have recognized in the mangled features the beautiful face of Hector.

[1] Tales of Ancient Greece. "Achilleus."

595. Did this appease the wrath of Achilles?

No. The death of Hector, and the restoration of Briseis, pure as when she had been taken away, would not satisfy him. His vow must be fulfilled, and the blood of twelve Trojan youths ran red on the altar of sacrifice in the funeral games of Patroclos.

596. What became of the body of Hector?

His father, the aged Priam, guided by Hermes, came to Achilles, and embracing his knees, prayed for the body of his child, over which Phœbus Apollo had spread his golden shield to keep away all unseemly things. So the body of Hector was borne back to Ilion, where his wife Andromache bitterly bemoaned her loss, and all the Trojans wept for him who had fought for them so bravely.

597. What is the sequel of the story?

At this point the poem called the Iliad comes to an end; but from the Odyssey we learn that Achilles was slain by Paris and Phœbus Apollo at the Skaian or western gates, and that Thetis, with her sea-nymphs, rose from the water and wrapped his body in shining robes, and after many days the Achaians placed it on a funeral-pile. His ashes were laid in a golden urn wrought by Hephæstus, and over it a great cairn was raised, that men might see it afar off as they sailed on the broad Hellespontos.

598. What does the name "broad" applied to the Hellespont show us?

That the Hellespontos of the Iliad is not the narrow strait between Sestos and Abydos, but the name of a wide sea, so called probably from a people named Helli or Selli, who lived on its shores, or crossed it in their migration from the east to the west.

599. Was the death of Achilles the end of the war?

No. The Achaians had still to fight on until the tenth year was completed. They then took Ilion and burnt it, and Priam and his people were slain. Paris himself, smitten with the poisoned arrows of Philoctetes, fled to Ida, where, as he lay dying, Œnone appeared before him, beautiful and loving as ever. But though her love might soothe him, it could not heal a wound made by the weapons of Heracles. So Paris died on Ida, and Œnone also died upon his funeral pile.

600. What is this wonderful siege of Troy?

It is "a repetition of the daily siege of the east by the solar powers that every evening are robbed of their brightest treasures in the west."

601. What is the treasure stolen in the Iliad?

Helen, whose name is the same as the Indian Saramâ, the dawn, from which the name Hermeias or Hermes is likewise derived.

602. Is the name of Paris also found in the old Sanskrit poems?

Yes; he is there called Pani, the deceiver, who, when Saramâ comes seeking the cows of Indra, beseeches her to remain with him. This Saramâ refuses, but she accepts from him a drink of milk; this passing disobedience of Saramâ to the commands given to her, is the germ of that unfaithfulness of Helen which causes the Trojan war.

603. Are any other names common to the Greek and Indian legends?

Yes. Achilles is the solar hero Aharyu; while Briseis, who is one of the first captives taken by the Achaians, is the offspring of Brisaya, conquered by the bright powers, in the Veda, *before* they can recover the treasures stolen by Pani.

604. What is especially remarkable in this tale of the Trojan war?

The blending of different ideas. For, as stealing Helen from the western Sparta, or as abetting in this theft, Paris and all the Trojans represent the dark powers of night who steal away the beautiful twilight from the western sky. But in the lives of many of the Trojan chiefs, as in that of Paris himself, we have a repetition of the life of Meleagros, Sigurd, and other solar heroes.

605. In what respects do they resemble each other?

As Heracles is compelled to serve Eurystheus, and Perseus has to do the bidding of Polydectes, so Achilles declares that he fights in no quarrel of his own, and that all the spoils won by his spear go to Agamemnon and his allies. Like Phœbus, Perseus, Theseus, and others, he has an unerring spear, and his sword slays all on whom it falls. He loves Briseis, but is soon parted from her, as Sigurd is parted from Brynhild.

606. What is the vow of Achilles when Briseis is taken from him?

Achilles swears to help the Achaians no longer: in other words, the sun hides his face behind the dark cloud; and as the golden rays are no longer seen when the face of the sun is hidden, so the Myrmidons no longer appear on the battle-field when their chief hangs up his spear and shield within his tent.

607. Why are the Myrmidons compared to wolves?

For the same reason which suggested the idea that Lycaon and his sons were changed into wolves. The Greek word Lukoi, *wolves*, is the same in sound with Leukoi, *brilliant;* and as the rays of the sun would be called Leukoi, so, when the meaning of the phrase had been in part forgotten, the Myrmidons, who are simply the sun's rays, were compared to wolves, with gleaming eyes and blood-red jaws.

608. What is Patroclos?

A feeble reflection of the splendor of Achilles, and standing to him precisely in the relation of Phaethon to Helios, or of Telemachus to Odysseus.

609. How is this shown?

As Phaethon must not whip the horses of Helios, so Patroclos must not drive the horses of Achilles on any other path than that which has been pointed out to him. Both disobey, and both are slain.

610. What is the struggle which follows the death of Patroclos?

The battle which the clouds fight over the sun, whose light they have for a time put out.

611. What is the vengeance of Achilles?

The victory of the sun, when, at the end of a stormy day, he comes forth from the mists and tramples on the clouds which have veiled his splendors. The streams of human blood poured on the altar of sacrifice are the torn and crimsoned clouds which stream up into the purple heaven at eventide.

612. Why is the body of Patroclos preserved from corruption?

Because, although Heracles may die in the arms of Iolê, the tale always speaks of them as conquerors in the end over the powers which seem to subdue them; and hence Thetis assures Achilles that even if Patroclos lay unburied for a year, his face should wear at its close a more glorious and touching beauty.

613. What is the restoration of Briseis?

It is the return of Iolê to Heracles, of Œnono to Paris, and of Brynhild to Sigurd.

614. What is the conflict which precedes the death of Hector?

The mighty battle of the vapors and the sun, who seems to trample on the darkness, just as Achilles tramples on the body of Hector: and as this victory of the sun is gained just as he is sinking into the sea, so the death of Achilles is said to follow very soon after that of Hector.

615. On the death of Achilles, the Trojans and Achaians are said to fight furiously over his body. Why is this?

Because the idea which suggested this story

is that of a stormy evening, when the clouds seem to fight over the dead sun.

616. What have we to learn from all this?

That the chief incidents of the story, and even the main features in the character of the chief heroes, were handed down ready-made for the Homeric poets. They might leave out this or that incident, but they were not free to alter the character of any. Thus they must describe Achilles as fighting in a quarrel which was not his own,—as robbed of Briseis,—as furious with rage and grief at her loss,—as hiding himself in his tent,—as sending out Patroclos instead of appearing himself in the battle-field,—as shedding the blood of human victims near the funeral pile of his friend,—and as dying early after his bright but troubled career.

617. Does this fact explain any thing further?

It explains the whole character of Achilles, which, regarded as that of an Achaian chief, is untrue, not only to their national character, but to human nature. His character, as drawn in the Iliad, is not only not Achaian, it is inhuman. There is no evidence that Achaian chiefs visited on the innocent the wrong-doings of the guilty; that they had no sense of duty, and no sympathy for the sufferings of those who had never injured them; that they offered human sacrifices, or that they mangled the corpses of brave enemies whom they had slain. But, although we have no evidence that Achaian chiefs ever did such things, such stories could not fail to spring up when phrases which had at first denoted only the varying action of the sun were regarded as relating the deeds of human beings.

THE RETURN OF THE HEROES FROM TROY.

618. What is the return of the heroes from Troy?

An event answering precisely to the return of Jason and his comrades from Colchis. These bring back the golden fleece, as Menelaüs returns with Helen to Sparta.

619. Are these legends uniform and consistent?

Only so far as they represent the heroes returning from the east to the west. Otherwise the incidents, and the names of persons and places, are changed almost at will. The tombs of Odysseus, Æneas, and many others, were shown in many and different places, for it was as easy to take them to one country as to another.

620. Who is the most important of these returning chieftains?

Odysseus, the tale of whose wanderings is given in the Odyssey, and whose story exactly reproduces that of Heracles and Perseus.

621. Why should this be so?

Because the return from Troy to Achaia represents the journey of the day from the east to the west.

622. How can this be shown?

As Indra soon loses sight of Dahana, as Œdipus in his infancy is parted from Iocaste, as Sigurd has to leave Brynhild almost as soon as he wins her, as Orpheus is parted from Eurydice, and Achilles from Briseis, so Odysseus soon after wedding Penelope has to leave her, in order to go to the Trojan war; and when Helen is won back from Paris, he journeys again, like the sun, from the east to his home in the west.

623. What is the character of his journey?

It is full of strange changes of happiness and misery, of successes and reverses, ending in complete victory, as the lights and shadows of a stormy and gloomy day are often scattered by the sun, whose glory they have so long hidden.

624. What do we gather from this?

That Odysseus is a counterpart of Achilles, whose career is repeated substantially in that of the chief of Ithaca, the main difference being that Achilles is as the sun in his strength, while the character of Odysseus is that of Phœbus, Asklepios, Iamus, and Medea, the possessors of a marvellous and superhuman wisdom.

625. What is the leading idea in the mind of Odysseus?

An intense desire and yearning to be united again with his wife, whom he left long ago in the bloom of her youthful beauty. Thus, although as he journeys homeward he is often tempted to tarry in his course, he cannot be made to give up his purpose.

626. Why is this?

Because Helios or the Sun cannot turn aside from the course marked out for him, whether in his daily or his yearly round.

627. What were the first dangers encountered by Odysseus on his return to Ithaca?

His first conflict was with a people called Kikones (Cicones), of Ismarus, who destroyed six men out of every ship in his fleet. Thence he came to the land of the Lotophagi, who spend their life in a delicious dream, eating the fruit of the lotos, which makes all who taste it forget their homes. Here Odysseus had to bind some of his men, who disobeyed his warning not to touch the fruit, and to drag them away to their ships. A terrible storm next carried him to the land of the Cyclopes, giants with a single eye in the midst of their foreheads.

628. What was his adventure in this region?

With several of his companions, Odysseus entered a cave in which were stored up large supplies of milk and cheese; but before they could make their escape, the Cyclops Polyphemus, son of Poseidon, entered and shut the entrance with a great rock which they could not move. The fire which he lit showed the forms of Odysseus and his men, two of whom Polyphemus cooked and devoured. After some more had been thus eaten, Odysseus and his men blinded the Cyclops by thrusting a burning fir-pole into his eye; and then tying his men under the rams of the Cyclops, he made his escape with them when Polyphemus opened the door of the cave.¹

629. How did he escape the other giants?

When Polyphemus asked his name, Odysseus told him that it was Outis, or Nobody. Hence when the other Cyclopes came to ask Polyphemus why he roared so loud, he told them that Nobody was doing him harm, and they, thinking that there was nothing the matter, went away to their own homes.

630. What was his next adventure?

Having escaped with difficulty from the cannibal Læstrygonians, he came to Ææa, where the lady Kirke (Circe) turned many of his men

---

¹ Tales of Ancient Greece. "Odysseus and Polyphemus."

into swine, but was compelled to restore them to their human shape by Odysseus, who had received from Hermes an herb which made the charms of Kirke powerless.[1]

631. Were his dangers now ended?

No. Kirke warned him against greater perils from the Seirens, who sate in their cool green caves, enticing the passing mariners to come and rest and forget all their toil and trouble.[2] They who yielded to the spell of their sweet music were dashed to pieces on the rocks. Odysseus therefore stuffed his sailors' ears with wax, but as he wished to hear their song, he had himself bound tightly to the mast; and thus he was carried safely past the danger, although he struggled hard to get free, as the echoes of their lulling music rose softly through the hot and breathless air. After this he lost many men, who were devoured by the two monsters Skylla (Scylla) and Charybdis, who sucked them down in their horrid whirlpools. The rest were lost in a storm after they had slain some of the cattle of Helios, whom Phaethusa and Lampetie, the *bright* and *glistening* daughters of the early Morning, tended in Thrinakia;[3] and Odys-

[1] Tales of Ancient Greece. "Odysseus and Kirke."
[2] Ibid. "Odysseus and the Seirens." [3] Ibid. "The Cattle of Helios."

seus, after tossing about for hours on the heaving sea, was thrown half dead on the shore of Ogygia. Here the beautiful Calypso[1] tended him lovingly in her cave, and kept him there seven years, although he longed once again to be at home. At length Hermes commanded her to let him go, and she then helped him to build a raft which carried him some way across the sea; but another storm washed him off, and he was thrown bleeding and senseless on the shore of Phæakia.

632. What next happened to him?

On coming to himself he heard the merry voices of girls who were playing on the beach while the clothes which they washed were drying. They were maidens who had come with Nausicaa, the beautiful daughter of king Alkinoüs and his wife Arêtê. Guided by her, Odysseus came to her father's palace, which stood in a glorious garden where the leaves never faded and the fruits glistened on the branches the whole year round. But more lovely than all was Nausicaa in her gentleness and purity.[2] Here Odysseus was kindly tended, and the king offered him his daughter as a wife; but Odys-

[1] Tales of Ancient Greece. "Odysseus and Kalypso."
[2] Ibid. "Odysseus and Nauseikâ."

seus had only one longing, which was once more to see Penelope after his long absence of twenty years, and so he was brought in a Phæakian ship to the shore of Ithaca, where he landed alone and in disguise.

633. In what state did he find his home?

He learned from his swineherd Eumæus that his father Laertes was living in squalid misery; that a crowd of chiefs who came as suitors to Penelope had taken up their abode in his house, where some of his servants were in league with them to devour his substance; and that Penelope, having promised to give them an answer when her web was finished, put them off continually by undoing at night that portion of the web which she had woven during the day.

634. How did Odysseus act?

He entered his own hall disguised as a beggar, and when provoked by some of the suitors, he challenged them to stretch a bow which hung upon the wall. This was the bow of Odysseus, which he alone was able to stretch. Thus they strove in vain to bend it, but when the beggar put forth his hand to seize it, the thunder of Zeus was heard in the heaven, and the suitors began to fall beneath the unerring arrows; but Telemachus had left the chamber-door ajar, and many of the chiefs, seizing the weapons which they found there, pressed hard upon Odysseus. Odysseus himself they could not hurt, but Telemachus was wounded, though not mortally like Patroclos. At this crisis Athena came to his aid, and scared them with her dazzling Ægis. The corpses of the suitors were thrust away like refuse; but on the body of Melanthios, the son of Dolios, Odysseus wreaked his full rage, as Achilles trampled on the body of Hector. Lastly, he summoned all the women who had abetted the suitors, and hung them up on a beam across his great hall. He was then united again with Penelope, for whom he had made the beautiful bridal chamber long years ago, and here he rested after the great slaughter.

635. What other story does this tale closely resemble?

It is the counterpart of the vengeance of Achilleus. In both an excessive revenge is taken for a comparatively slight wrong. Indeed, in the case of Odysseus, the wrong was confined to the intrusion of the suitors into his house.

636. Is the character of Odysseus true to that of the Achaians, or historical Greeks?

We have no evidence whatever for thinking

that it was. It may be more justly called not only not Achaian, but inhuman. Odysseus uses poisoned arrows, he shoots a man behind his back and without warning, he tells lies whenever it suits his purpose to do so, he slays a whole band of chieftains who had done him no great injury, and then hangs up "like sparrows on a string" a crowd of women, simply because they had not resisted the demands of the suitors.

637. What have we to learn from this?

That only mischief can follow if we will insist on regarding as a human model a being whose story has grown up from the phrases which lie at the root of the story of Achilles.

638. Is the parallel between the two stories a close one?

It may be traced down to the minutest particulars. Both have weapons which they alone can wield, both are aided by Athena, both have in Patroclos and Telemachus a faint reflection of their own strength, both make a vow to exact a deadly vengeance, both trample on and disfigure their slaughtered enemy; both are nearly overpowered at one part of the struggle, and both have a time of quietness and rest after the fearful conflict.

639. Who is Penelope, and what is her web?

Penelope is the *weaver*, like Helios in the story of Medea; but her web, although often begun, cannot be finished until Odysseus returns, because the web of morning clouds reappears only at sundown.

640. What is the meaning of the name Odysseus?

When his old nurse Eurycleia recognizes him in the bath by the mark left on his leg by the bite of a boar in his early youth, she tells him that he received his name Odysseus to express the hatred generally felt for his grandfather Autolycus.

641. Is this interpretation correct?

The name may possibly be connected with a Greek verb (odussomai) meaning *to be angry;* but the way of accounting for it is worth nothing. The names explain themselves. Eurycleia, like Euryanassa, Europa, and many others, is simply a name for the dawn, who is the nurse of the sun; and the boar's wound is repeated exactly in the story of Adonis. The name Autolycus, again, like that of Lycaon, denotes simply light, while Odysseus is the angry sun, who hides himself behind the thick clouds. Thus disguised, he approaches his home, the darkness being greatest just before the beginning of the last strife.

642. Do any other names in the story explain themselves?

Many, if not most of them do. Thus Odysseus has a dog Argus (the white or shining), the same hound, in fact, which appears by the side of Artemis in the legend of Procris. The servants who aid the suitors have such names as Melanthius and Melantho, the *black*, the children of Dolios, the *treacherous* darkness; and the name of Telemachus, like those of Telephos and Telephassa, represents the far-shooting light of Phœbus Hecaergos.

643. What do we learn generally from such resemblances?

That the phrases which described the infinitely various aspects of the outer world furnished inexhaustible materials for legends which could be expanded into splendid epic poems. The Homeric poets worked with marvellous success on these materials, which also furnished the frame-work for the great epic poems of other countries,—this fact being proved by the astonishing coincidences, in minute incidents as well as in names and characters, between the Iliad and Odyssey, the Lay of the Nibelungs, and the Persian epic of Firdusi.

644. Are any historical facts mixed up with these tales of Paris, Helen, Achilles, and Odysseus?

We are not justified in thinking so. We know that most of the incidents belonging to these stories never could have taken place: we know that Aphrodite and Athena never mingled in battles with mortal men, and that the armor of no Achaian chief was ever forged on the anvil of Hephæstus. We may, if we please, strike out all the marvellous events in the story, and make up the account of a war without Thetis and Helen, or Sarpedon and Memnon, or Xanthos and Balios: we shall then have (as in the preface of Thucydides) the account of something which may have taken place, but which we have no warrant whatever for regarding as historical fact. The names and incidents of the myth belong to the beautiful cloud-land

Where Ilion, like a mist, rose into towers,[1]

and it is labor lost to search in Europe or Asia for the Phœnicia, Ortygia, Lycia, Phæakia, Delos, Thrinakia, Arcadia, and Ethiopia where Helios journeys in storm and calm, in splendor or in gloom, along the blue seas of heaven.

[1] Tennyson's Tithonus.

PAN.

INHABITANTS OF THE GREEK MYTHICAL WORLD.

645. Do the names already mentioned complete the list of beings noticed in the mythology of the Greeks?

No. In addition to the Olympian gods and the dynastic heroes of the Greek cities, there are very many names, some of which may be classed together, but which cannot be said to have any mythical history. Many of these are simply objects in the natural world, regarded as having the consciousness of human beings.

646. Mention some beings of this kind.

The Hamadryads, nymphs who were supposed to live and die with the trees to which they were attached; and the Oreads, or nymphs of the mountains.

647. Who were the Hyades?

Daughters of Atlas and Æthra, who is also mother of Theseus. They wept themselves to death, it is said, and form a cluster of stars which betoken rain.

648. Who were the Heliades?

Daughters of Helios, who wept tears of amber on the death of their brother Phaethon.

649. Who were the Gigantes, or giants?

In the Homeric poems, they are the Cyclopes who dwell in Thrinakia; in Hesiod, they are beings produced by the blood of Ouranos (heaven) falling on Gê (the earth). They answer to the Trolls, or frost giants of northern mythology.

650. Who were the Aloadæ?

Two giants, named Otos and Ephialtes, sons of Poseidon, were so called (from *olôe*, a threshing-floor), as possessing the strength of millstones.

651. What were the Moliones?

This name, meaning the *Grinders*, was given to Eurytus and Actor, sons of Poseidon. In character, they answer to the Thor Miölnir of Norse mythology.

652. Who was Boreas?

The son of Astræus and Eos, commonly known as the god of the north wind. His wife was Oreithyia, daughter of Erechtheus and sister of Procris.

653. What was Erebus?

The offspring of Chaos, who dwelt in the gloomy space through which the souls passed to Hades.

654. Who is Enyo?

In the theogony of Hesiod, she is one of the Graiæ. By others she is described as a goddess who accompanies Ares and delights in havoc and bloodshed. Ares himself is sometimes called Enyalios.

655. Who were the Harpies?

The storm winds, described in Hesiod as the beautiful daughters of Thaumas and Electra, but represented as loathsome beings in Virgil.

656. Who are the Muses?

Goddesses of music, poetry, art, and science. They seem at first to have been three in number, and afterward to have been increased to nine. They were also called Pierides, from Pieria, near Olympus; but another legend says, that the Pierides were daughters of Pieros, king of Emathia, who entering into a contest with the Muses, were beaten by them and changed into birds. The names of the nine Muses are, Cleio (*the proclaimer*), Euterpe (*the charmer*), Erato (*the lovely*), Thaleia (*the joyous*), Melpomene (*the singer*), Terpsichore (*the enjoyer of dances*), Polymnia (*the lover of songs*), Urania (*the heavenly*), and Calliope (*the beautiful voiced*).

657. Who was Orion?

A great hunter, loved by Artemis and Eos, and placed after his death among the stars.

658. What is Pallas?

A name given to Athena, probably as being the virgin goddess.

659. Who was Pan?

A deity who presided over flocks and herds, said by some to be a son of Hermes, born in Arcadia. He is represented with the head and breast of a man, and the lower parts of a goat. He is said to have journeyed through India with Dionysus, and, being once surrounded by enemies, to have been rescued by the shoutings of his men, who thus scared them away. Hence the word *panic* to denote any sudden and vague terror. The name Pan is akin to the Sanskrit word for wind, Pavana, and probably to the Latin, Favonius.

660. Who are the Pleiades?

Seven daughters of Atlas and Æthra who wept themselves to death for the loss of their sisters, the Hyades.

661. Who was Eros?

The god of love. In Hesiod, he is one of the primitive powers, along with Chaos, Gaia, and Tartarus. Later poets call him a son of Hermes, or of Ares, and of Artemis or Aphrodite.

662. Who was Proteus?

In the Odyssey, he is an old man who tends the seals of Poseidon, and rises at midday from the sea to sleep upon the shore. He had the power of changing himself into any form, like the "farmer Weathersky" of the Norse tales.

663. Who was Priapus?

He is called a son of Dionysus and Aphrodite, and was worshipped as the cause of fertility to fruits and flocks.

664. What was Psyche?

The word denotes the breath of living things; but, in the story of Eros and Psyche, she is a maiden who thinks that she is married to a monster, and who, taking a lamp to look at him, finds that he is beautiful, but a drop of oil falling from the lamp awakens Eros, who vanishes away. After years of sorrow and trouble Psyche is united to him again. The story is in part the same as that of Beauty and the Beast, and many other forms of it are given in Grimm's Household Tales.

665. Who was Zagreos?

Zagreos seems to be a name for Dionysus. He is described as the horned child of Zeus and Persephone.

666. Who was Hesperus?

The god of the western heaven and father of the Hesperides, who, with the dragon Ladon, guarded the golden apples of Hera.

667. Who were Castor and Polydeukes?

They are called the two Dioscûri, or sons of Zeus. In the Iliad and Odyssey they are brothers of Helen; but many other accounts are given of their parentage. By the Latins Polydeukes was called Pollux.

668. Who were the Cabeiri?

Mystic deities, said by some to be children of Hephæstus and Cabeira, daughter of Proteus.

669. Who were the Corybantes and Dactyli?

Beings, seemingly, of the same kind as the Cabeiri. The Corybantes are spoken of as sons of Apollo. The Phrygian priests of Cybele were called Dactyli.

670. Who was Cybele, or Kybele?

She is supposed to have been originally the Phrygian goddess of the earth. The Greeks identified her with Rhea, and the Latins with Ops.

671. Who was Hebe?

The goddess of youth, answering to the Latin Juventas.

672. Who was Hymen?

A Greek god of marriage, by some called a son of Apollo.

673. Who was Iris?

In the Homeric mythology Iris is, like Hermes, a messenger of the gods. In Hesiod she is a sister of the Harpies. According to others, she was the wife of Zephyrus (the west wind), and mother of Eos (the morning).

674. Who was Morpheus?

The shaper of dreams. He is called a son of Hupnos, *sleep*.

675. Who was Ganymedes?

He is described, in the Homeric mythology, as a beautiful Trojan youth, who was taken to be the cupbearer of Zeus on Olympus.

GREEK MYTHICAL PERSONAGES. 235

676. Who was Laocoon?

A priest of Apollo, who tried to dissuade the Trojans from admitting the wooden horse within the walls of Troy. Athena therefore sent two serpents who crushed him and his sons within their monstrous folds.

677. Who was Silenus?

An attendant of Dionysus, and leader of the Satyrs, beings who, like Pan, are represented as having human heads, arms, and breasts, with the lower parts of goats.

678. Who was Charon?

The ferryman who conducted the souls of the dead across the Stygian lake to the judgment-seat of Minos, Rhadamanthus, and Æacus. He is called a son of Erebus.

679. Name the rivers of Hades.

Acheron, Kokutos (Cocytus), Styx, Phlegethon or Pyriphlegethon, and Lethe.

680. What is the meaning of these names?

Acheron (like Achelous, Axius, Axe, Exe, Usk, and very many others) means only *water*. Kôkûtos is the river of groans and tears; Styx is the hateful stream; Phlegethon or Pyriphlegethon the river of fire; and Lethe belongs, like Leto, and Leda the mother of the Dioscuri, to the land of Latmos, or forgetfulness and death.

681. Who was Kekrops or Cecrops?

The mythical founder of Athens, who is described as an autochthon, or indigenous hero, the upper part of his body being human, and the lower parts those of a dragon. Herse, the *dew*, is assigned to him as a daughter. He is, in short, the counterpart of Erechtheus. The fancies of a comparatively late age brought him from Sais in Egypt; but there is nothing in the Greek mythology which points to any connection with that country during the mythopœic (or myth-making) ages.

LATIN MYTHOLOGY.

682. Does the mythology of the Latins and Romans correspond to that of the Greeks?

The so-called Latin mythology of the age of Virgil and Horace is a mere copy of the Greek, and, therefore, can scarcely be regarded as Latin at all.

683. Was there, then, a Latin mythology which was not borrowed in this way?

Yes. Before the Latin tribes had any intercourse with the Greeks, they had their own deities and supernatural beings, whose character attests the worship of a people employed chiefly in tilling the earth. These deities had their names, with certain qualities or dispositions attached to them; but few or no stories were told about them, and hence, when they were thrown with Greek settlers, they were tempted first to identify the Latin gods with those of the Greeks, and then to transfer to the Latin deities all the legends which the Greeks related of their own mythical beings.

684. In so doing did they introduce any new features?

Very rarely. They were generally content

with assigning all the Greek legends to Latin gods, with which, in most cases, they had neither names nor qualities in common; and thus the stories told of Hermes were related also of Mercury. But in one or two instances the character of the Greek deity is altered for the worse. Thus, as the lovely Saranyu, or dawn, of India, became the dark and stern Erinys of the Greeks, so the Harpies, who in the Hesiodic poems are the beautiful daughters of Thaumas and Electra, are in Virgil foul birds of prey.

JUPITER.

685. What is Jupiter?

This name, which corresponds exactly to the Zeus-patêr of the Greek and the Dyaus-pitar of the Hindu, denotes the Supreme God; but with the earlier Latins no mythical tales were attached to it, as in the Greek mythology.

686. Did the word still retain with them its original meaning of heaven, or sky?

Yes: they spoke of being "under the cool, or clear Jove;" and his Oscan name Lucerius, or Lucesius (akin to Lykegenes, as a name for Phœbus), points to the bright shining firmament.

687. Had Jupiter, then, many names?

He was invoked under different epithets, according to the matter for which his aid was needed. Thus, as calling down lightning, he was Jupiter Elicius; as giving rain, Jupiter Pluvius; as protecting boundaries, Jupiter Terminus, the Zeus Horios of the Greeks.

688. Who was the wife of Jupiter?

She is called Juno, a name which would answer to a Greek form Zenon, as a feminine.

689. Are there any Latin stories about Juno?

No. Those which are told of her by later poets were borrowed from the Greek.

690. How was Juno addressed?

Like Jupiter, by many names. Thus, as queen of heaven, she was Juno Regina; as presiding over marriage, Juno Jugalis; and as guarding money and treasure, Juno Moneta, a name which probably comes from the same root with Minerva.

NEPTUNE.

691. Who was Neptune?

The later Romans identified him with the Greek Poseidon, but in character he answers more nearly to Nereus. He is the god who dwells on the waters, and his name is connected with many words which mean to *bathe,* or *swim.*

PLUTO.

692. What is Pluto?

A Greek name for Hades, as the guardian of the hidden treasures of the earth. Another name given to him by the Latins was Dis, which was regarded as a shortened form of Dives, *rich;* but this name is probably connected with Deus, Divus, the Greek Theos, and the Indian Dyaus. The name of his wife, Proserpina, is only another form of the Greek Persephonê.

VESTA.

693. Who is Vesta?

A deity who, in name as well as in character, answers precisely to the Greek Hestia. This goddess is probably part of the common inheritance brought by the ancestors of the Greek and Latin tribes from the home where they had once dwelt together. Vesta with the Romans was a goddess of far greater importance than

Hestia among the Greeks, her fire being kept up by the Vestal virgins, who were consecrated to her service.

CERES.

694. What is Ceres?

A name applied to the Earth, as the producer of fruits. Hence she was identified with the Greek Demeter. The word has been regarded by some as meaning *the maker;* others see in it only another form of the Greek Cora, or Korê *(the maiden),* a name of Persephonê. It is probably derived from the same root which yields the Sanskrit *śarad,* autumn (viz. *śri,* or *srî,* to cook, to ripen).

MINERVA.

695. What is the meaning of the name Minerva?

Like the Latin *mens,* the Greek *ménos,* and the English *mind,* it denotes *thought* or *wisdom ;* it is also connected with the Latin *Mane,* the morning, and *Matuta,* the dawn. Hence the idea of Minerva is far higher than that of the Greek Athena, with whom she was identified.

696. Is the germ of this idea found in any other mythology?

Yes. In the Vedic hymns the dawn is spoken of as waking every mortal to walk about, and receiving praise from every *thinker*. As such, she is strictly the *Moneta*, a name which the Romans applied to Juno.

MARS.

697. What is Mars?

The Latin god of war; but although he was identified with the Greek Arês, and although the names belong to the same root, yet the idea of the Latin Mars is far the higher and more dignified of the two.

698. Are there any other forms of this name?

Yes. By the Oscans and Sabines he was called Mamers; and the Roman form Mars is a contraction of Mavors or Mavers.

699. Are any legends related of this god?

He is spoken of as the father of Romulus and Remus, the mythical founders of Rome.

700. What were Romulus and Remus?

Twin sons of the vestal Ilia; but the two names are different forms of the same word.

The stories about these brothers agree closely with those which are related of Œdipus, Telephus, and other heroes.

701. Is there, then, nothing historical in the story of Romulus?

We have no reason for thinking otherwise. He is simply the Eponymus of Rome—in other words, a being invented to account for the name of a city, just as Pelasgus, Lelex, Sparta, Orchomenos, and a host of others were invented by the Greeks. Like Heracles and other heroes, he vanishes away in a storm of thunder and lightning; and thenceforth he is said to have been worshipped under the name Quirinus.

VENUS.

702. What is Venus?

The Latin goddess of beauty and love, to whom were transferred all the stories told of the Greek Aphrodite. As the latter was said to be mother of Æneas, the ancestor of Romulus, so Venus was supposed to be the special protector of the Roman state.

703. What is the origin of the name?

It comes from a root which signifies *favor;*

and is found in the Latin word *venia*, grace or pardon, as well as in *venerate* and *winsome*.

VULCAN.

704. What is Vulcan?

The Latin god of fire, who was identified with the Greek Hephæstus. Hence he is called the husband of Venus. The name is akin to the Sanskrit *ulkâ*, a firebrand, a meteor.

APOLLO.

705. Is Apollo or Phœbus Apollo a Latin god?

No. The name is borrowed from the Greeks, and all that is related of him is Greek also. Thus the name of his mother Latona is only a Latin form of the Greek Leto, which again is only another form of the name of Leda, the mother of the Dioscuri. The idea of the god of light is expressed in the word Lucerius, or Lucesius, the old Oscan name for Jupiter.

DIANA AND JANUS.

706. What is Diana?

The feminine form of the name Dianus, or

Janus, which, again, is akin to Juno, the Greek Zeus, and the Sanskrit Dyaus, the sky. She was identified with the Greek Artemis, and is, therefore, called a sister of Apollo.

707. What is Janus or Dianus?

By the Romans he was represented as having two faces, which looked opposite ways—a notion which arose from their mistakenly connecting the word with *dis, duo (two)*, words denoting division. The gate of Janus at Rome was kept open in time of war and shut in time of peace; and it is said to have been closed only six times in eight hundred years.

MERCURY.

708. Who was Mercury?

A Latin god of traffic and gain, from *merx, commerce*. He was identified with the Greek Hermes, to whom he bears no resemblance; and the Roman Fetials, or heralds, refused to allow that they were both the same god.

ÆSCULAPIUS.

709. Is Æsculapius a Latin god?

No. The name, which is another form of

Asklepios, is, with the character and mythical history of the god, imported bodily from Greek mythology.

BACCHUS.

710. Who is Bacchus?

The same as the Greek god Dionysus, who was also called Iacchos or Bacchus, perhaps (as some have thought) from the cries and shouts with which he was worshipped.

HERCULES.

711. Who is Hercules?

As a Latin god he seems to have been connected with boundaries, or fences, like Jupiter Terminus, the Zeus Horios of the Greeks; and as such, his name was probably Herclus or Herculus. But the similarity of the name led the Romans to identify their Herculus with the Greek Heracles. They were further strengthened in this conclusion by the fact that a hero, named Garanus, or Recaranus, was said to have slain a great robber named Cacus, and that this hero closely resembled not only Heracles, but

Perseus, Theseus, Œdipus, and all other destroyers of monsters and evil-doers.

712. *What is the story of Cacus?*

It is told in many ways; but the most popular version says that when Hercules reached the banks of the Tiber, Cacus, the three-headed son of Vulcan, stole some of his cattle, and, to avoid detection, dragged them backward into his cave. But their lowing reached the ears of Hercules, who, forcing his way into the robber's den, recovered not only his cattle, but all the stolen treasures which had been stored within it. In vain Cacus vomited forth smoke and flame upon his enemy, who soon slew him with his unerring darts.

713. *Can the growth of this story be accounted for?*

It is only another form of the many tales which recount the conflict of the heaven or the sun with the powers of night and darkness. Recaranus, who kills the monster, is like Sancus, whose name was also inscribed on the Ara Maxima, or great altar of Hercules, simply Jupiter,—so called as being the maker or creator, the name Recaranus being thus, as some have thought, connected with that of Ceres.

714. *What, then, is Cacus?*

As the three-headed monster, he answers exactly to the Greek Geryon and Kerberos (Cerberus), the Indian Sarvara. As stealing the cows of Hercules, he is Vritra, who shuts up the rain in the thunder-cloud, and who is pierced by the lance of Indra. He is again seen in the Panis who steals the cows of Indra. The flames which he sends forth from his cave are the lightnings which precede that down-pour of the rain which is signified by the recovery of the cows from Cacus.

715. What is the origin of the name Cacus?

By some it has been connected with the Greek word kakos, *bad*. But the length of the first syllable is against this notion. Other forms of the name are Kakias and Cæculus, who, in the mythology of Præneste, a town near Rome, was a son of Vulcan, and also a flame-vomiting robber. Now Aristotle speaks of a wind called Kaikias (Cæcias) which has the power of attracting the clouds, and cites the proverb that men draw mischiefs toward themselves as Kaikias draws the clouds. But the clouds are everywhere the cattle or cows of Indra, Helios, Phœbus, and Heracles: hence the proverb would become a tale which would have its germ in the phrase " Cæculus is stealing the cows of

Hercules." The combat which follows is that struggle of Indra with Vritra which ends with the victory of the powers of light.

SATURN.

716. What is Saturn?

A Latin god who has been identified with the Greek Cronos, with whom he has no features in common. The name denotes one who sows seed, and Saturn thus answers more nearly to the Greek Triptolemus. His wife, Ops, a goddess of wealth or fertility, was, with no better reason, identified with Rhea. As Saturn was said to have vanished from the earth when his work was done, it was thought that the land of Latium received its name as being his hiding-place.

717. What is the origin of the name Latium?

It is the country of the Latini or Lavini, whose name is identified by Niebuhr (in his History of Rome) with that of the Daunii and the Danai, who follow Agamemnon to Troy.

AURORA.

718. Who was Aurora?

The goddess of morning, identified with the Greek Eos, the wife of Tithonos.

719. Does the name correspond to any in Eastern mythology?

It is connected with the Sanskrit Ushas, a name for the dawn, from a root which is common to the Latin aurum, *gold*, and urere, *to burn*.

AVERNUS.

720. What was Avernus?

This name was given to an Italian lake near Naples, which was supposed to be the entrance to the infernal regions. The Cumæan Sibyl lived in a cave near its shores.

721. Is the name a Latin one?

No; it is only a Latinized form of the Greek Aornos, which denotes a place without birds. It was thought that none could fly over it, owing to the deadly vapors which rose from its surface.

POMONA

LATIN DEITIES NOT IDENTIFIED WITH GREEK GODS.

722. What were the Lares?

Domestic deities. They seem to have been regarded as the souls of deceased ancestors. There were Lares not only of families, but of the city, the country, the roads.

723. Are the Lares connected with any other Latin deities?

They form part of the class known as Penates, or household gods, whose name seems to be derived from *penus*, a store of food. There were public as well as private Penates.

724. Are the Lares known under any other name?

They are commonly addressed as the Manes, a general name for the spirits of the dead. This word means "the good ones," and recurs in the name of Mana, an Italian goddess, and in the word *immanis,* cruel.

725. Were they ever described in any other way?

Those spirits which were supposed to be capable of injuring the living were called Lemures. The spectres of the dead generally were named Larvæ.

726. Who were the Palici?

Twin deities worshipped in Sicily, of whom little more is known than the name, which may possibly be connected with that of Pales, a rural deity worshipped especially by shepherds.

727. What were the Parcæ?

According to later poets, they are three sisters who were identified with the Greek Mœræ, Clotho, Lachesis, and Atropos.

728. What were the Fates?

The name was used to denote the Parcæ. The word fatum, *fate,* means *a thing spoken,* and answers to the Aisa of the Greeks, which is the spoken word of Zeus, *i. e.,* Necessity or Destiny.

729. What were the Genii?

Superhuman beings, whose life, according to

the belief of the old Italian races, ceased with that of the persons whom they guarded.

730. Who were the Dii Indigetes?

The Latin title for those mythical heroes of the land who after their deaths were ranked among the gods.

731. What were the Dii Consentes?

A name (denoting agreement or harmony) which in later times was supposed to denote the twelve Olympian gods. Originally they consisted of six male and six female deities, whose names cannot be determined with certainty.

732. Who was Bellona?

The Latin goddess of war (bellum).

733. Who was the Bona Dea, or good goddess?

She is described as a sister or daughter of Faunus, worshipped only by women. She is herself called Fauna; but Fauna and Faunus mean simply the *favorer*, and were rural deities of the old Latins.

734. Who were the Camenæ?

Deities whose name, in the form Carmentes and Carmenæ, connects them with *carmen*, a song. Hence they were identified with the Greek muses.

735. Who was Egeria?

One of the Camenæ, who is said to have been the secret counsellor of the mythical king Numa.

736. Who was Laverna?

The patron goddess of thieves.

737. Who were Pilumnus, Picumnus, and Semo Sancus?

Pilumnus and Picumnus were two brothers, worshipped as rural deities. The names are mere epithets, Pilumnus being the grinder of corn, and Picumnus the tiller of the earth. The names Semo Sancus are sometimes taken together to denote the same deity. They are really two, Sancus being the ratifier of oaths or contracts, and Semo the sower of seed.

738. Who was Pomona?

The Latin goddess of fruits and fruit-trees. She is said to have been loved by Silvanus, a deity of the woods, by Picus (who, like Picumnus, is the tiller of the ground), and by Vertumnus, the god of the changing seasons.

739. Who was Anna Perenna?

The giver of plenty in the returning seasons of the year. She was identified by late poets with Anna, the sister of Dido, the mythical foundress of Carthage.

740. Who was Consus?

A deity of whom little more is known than that the festival called Consualia was celebrated in his honor. The name may be connected with that of the Consentes Dii.

741. Who are Gradivus and Mulciber?

Gradivus is a name of Mars, as the *strider*, and Mulciber of Vulcan, as *softening* the heated iron.

742. What is Favonius?

A name for the west or southwest wind, called Zephyros (the Zephyr) by the Greeks.

OSIRIS.

EGYPTIAN MYTHOLOGY.

743. What is the character of Egyptian mythology?

Some of the Egyptian myths seem to have a more direct reference to facts of astronomy than may be found generally in Greek mythology; but there is no doubt that, like the Greek myths, those of the Egyptians had their foundation in phrases which described the sights and objects of the outward world.

744. Is there any connection between the Greek and Egyptian systems of mythology?

They grew up quite independently of each other; and the mythology of the Homeric and

Hesiodic poems exhibits no traces of the influence of Egyptian thought. But after Egypt had been thrown open to Greek commerce, the Greeks (like the first English who studied Sanskrit in India,) were so impressed with the grandeur of the country and the elaborate mysticism of the priesthood, that they were tempted not only to identify their own deities with those of Egypt, but to fancy that their names, as well as the actions ascribed to them, were derived from Egypt.

745. How did this mystical system of the Egyptian priests grow up?

It was grafted in the process of ages on simpler myths, which corresponded essentially to the phrases which lie at the root of Hindu, Greek, and Teutonic mythology. Thus the sleep of Osiris during the winter, before his reappearance in the spring, is the sleep of the fair maiden who is waked up by Sigurd, and answers to the imprisonment of Korê or Persephone in Hades.

746. Who was Ammon?

The god so called by the Greeks (who connected the name with the sand, *ammos*, with which his temple in the Oasis was surrounded), is the Egyptian Amen-ra, or Kneph, the ram-headed and horned god, who reappears in the Orphic Zagreos.

747. What was Anubis?

A being represented with the head of a dog, or jackal, and said to be the companion of Osiris and Isis.

748. Who were Isis and Osiris?

Isis is called the wife of Osiris and mother of Horus, and seems to have been at first the goddess of the earth, like the Greek Dêmêter. She was represented as a woman with the horns of a cow. Osiris, her husband or son (for he is regarded as both), is killed by his brother Set or Sethi, a being whose character answers to that of the Hindu Vritra; but after his imprisonment beneath the earth, he rises to a new life, and becomes the judge of the dead. His chief sanctuary was in the island of Philæ.

749. Who was Horus?

The son of Isis, represented as a boy sitting on a lotus-flower, with a finger in his mouth. His name, Har-pi-chruti, *Horus the child*, was thrown into the form of Harpocrates by the Greeks.

750. What was Apis?

The calf-god, who was supposed to manifest

himself from time to time in a bull, which was recognized by certain signs. This bull was then consecrated, and received high worship. It was not suffered to live more than twenty-five years, and his burial was followed by a general mourning, until a new calf with the proper marks was discovered. This god the Greeks identified with Epaphus, the child of Io.

751. What was Serapis?

It is said to have been a name given to Apis after his death and deification.

752. What was Neith?

A deity represented as covered with a veil, and identified by the Greeks (without any reason) with their goddess Athena. She is often associated with Phthah, the pygmy god.

753. What was Ra?

The name under which the sun was worshipped by the Egyptians.

754. What was the Phœnix?

According to the historian Herodotus, it was a bird which the Egyptians regarded as the emblem of immortality; but Herodotus says nothing of the resurrection of the Phœnix from its own ashes, while others, instead of saying that a new Phœnix sprung full-grown from the funeral pile of the old one, spoke of a worm which came out from the dead body, and gradually grew into another Phœnix.

ISIS AND HORUS.

ASSYRIAN MYTHOLOGY.

755. What are the Assyrian deities?

Deities whose names were, for the most part, at first mere epithets of the sun, but came in course of time to denote different gods. Thus the sun was worshipped as Bel or Baal, the Lord, and as Moloch, or the King, these names being gradually set apart for separate deities, just as Endymion, Hyperion, Apollo, Perseus, all originally mere names of Helios (the sun), became at length names of different persons.

756. Where was the sun chiefly worshipped as Baal?

In Babylon. His worship was also introduced by Ahab into the kingdom of Israel.

757. What people were most widely known for their devotion to Moloch?

The Phœnicians, who appeased him with the blood of infants, especially of the first-born. Carthage was noted for these horrid sacrifices; five hundred children, it is said, were placed at once in the fiery jaws of the idol, when the Sicilian Agathocles was about to attack the city.

758. Was the worship of Moloch practised by the Jews?

Yes; with great persistency, down to the time

of the Babylonish captivity. The prophets constantly denounce the wrath of God on the abominable human sacrifices which were offered up in the valley of Hinnom, to the east of Jerusalem.

759. Does the name appear in any other form?

Yes; in Milcom, the Ammonite god, and in the names of Adrammelech and Anammelech, gods of Sepharvaim.

760. Who was Chemosh?

The god of the Moabites. The name is, perhaps, only another form of the Hebrew Shemesh and the Assyrian Shamas, the sun.

761. What was Nebo?

A Babylonian deity, whose name is found in that of Nebuchadnezzar, and other kings.

762. Who was Ishtar?

A goddess resembling most nearly the Aphrodite of the Greeks, who spoke of her as Astarte. In the Old Testament she is called Ashtaroth.

763. Who was Tammuz?

A beautiful youth, known also as Adonis, the *lord*, for whose death the women mourned in the autumn-time. The same idea is found in the mythical tales of Osiris and Persephone.

764. Who was Xisuthrus?

He is said to have been a just man, who, with

other righteous men, was saved in an ark from a great flood which overwhelmed the whole of Babylonia.

765. What was Oannes?

The fish-god of the Babylonians. This being, who was represented with a human form behind which appeared the scaly covering of a fish, was said to dwell in the sea, out of which he came every day to teach the Babylonians all wisdom and science. By the Philistines he was worshipped under the name Dagon. As emerging daily from the sea, and as possessed of a mysterious wisdom, he is manifestly the same as the Greek Proteus.

TRIMOURTI.

THE MYTHOLOGY OF THE VEDA.

766. For what reason is the Vedic or earliest Hindu mythology especially valuable?

As furnishing a key to that of the Persians, Greeks, Latins, Romans, and other races. Thus names by which the Greeks denoted different gods and heroes, are in the Vedas mere epithets the meaning of which cannot be mistaken; and the most complicated legends can be traced to their germ in some phrase which in these most ancient of all poems described simply some incident or phenomenon in the course of the outward world.

767. Mention some instances of this process.

In the Veda, Arjuni, Brisaya, Dahana, Ushas, Sarama, and Saranyu, are names for the morning light: for the Greeks they were separate beings whom they knew as Argynnis, Briseis, Daphne, Eos, Helen, and Erinys. In the same way the Vedas spoke of the Panis as tempting Sarama to be unfaithful; for the Greeks, this phrase had grown into the stealing away of Helen by Paris, and the complicated legend of the war of Troy.

768. Is the earlier Hindu mythology to be distinguished from that of later times?

Yes: the later mythology is as intricate as the earlier is simple; but the way in which the system has been developed in India throws the clearest light on the same process, as it has gone on in other countries. Thus, in the oldest poems there are no genealogies or settled marriages among the gods. The sister in one legend is the wife or mother in another, and the same being is spoken of at different times as the son and brother of the same god.

769. What are the chief deities in these ancient hymns?

Perhaps the most important are Varuna, Agni, and Indra.

770. What is Varuna?

The broad heaven which is spread over and veils the earth. But many of the hymns addressed to Varuna are addressed to him simply as a name for the One God who has made and who governs all things.

771. Is Varuna found in Greek mythology?

Yes, as Ouranos (Uranus); but as in Greece, Zeus (the Sanskrit Dyaus) became the name for the supreme God, Ouranos lost his importance and almost faded out of sight.

772. Who is Agni?

The fire, which, when the fuel is kindled, steps forth like a war-horse from his prison, leaving a dark path (of smoke) behind him.

773. Is Agni found in Western mythology?

No; but the name is found in the Latin word ignis, *fire*.

774. Who is Indra?

The god of the clear heaven, and so of light, warmth, and fertilizing rain,—so named from a root denoting *moisture*, and thus answering to the Jupiter Pluvius of the Latins.

775. How is he chiefly represented?

As doing battle with Vritra, the enemy, who by shutting up the rain brings drought upon the earth.

776. How is Vritra described?

As a great dragon, smitten by the lance of Indra, as Python is pierced by that of Apollo. As such, he is called Ahi, which is the same as the Greek Echidna, and the Latin word anguis, *a snake*.

777. What other forms does Vritra assume in Western mythology?

It corresponds exactly to the Sphinx in the story of Œdipus, to the Libyan dragon slain by Perseus, to Fafnir slain by Sigurd, as well as to the many monsters slain by other heroes.

778. Is the name found in Greek legends?

Yes; it is the same as that of Orthros, who with Kerberos (Cerberus), the Vedic Sarvara, guards the gates of Hades, who answers to the Hindu Yama.

779. What are the Harits?

In the Vedic hymns they are the bright horses of the sun; in the West they became beautiful women, called by the Greeks Charites, by the Latins Gratiæ or Graces (from a root Ghar, *to shine*).

780. What are Trita and Traitana?

Names given to the god of the clear heaven. They reappear in the Greek Triton and Tritogenia.

781. What are the Maruts?

The storm winds, whose name (from mar, *to grind*) reappears in the Greek Ares, the Latin Mars, and Mors, *death*, and in the Teutonic Thor Miölnir, or the crusher.

782. Who are the Rishis?

Seven wise men who were supposed to dwell in the seven stars of the constellation which we call the Great Bear. These stars were called at first the seven Arkshas, or shiners; but as the word Rishi also comes from the same root, the two were confused together, just as in Greece they were converted into bears—the name arctoi, *bears*, belonging to the same root.

783. What are Bhuranyu and Pramantha?

The name Bhuranyu is the same as the Greek Phoroneus, while Pramantha answers to Prometheus.

784. What is Ushas?

A name for the dawn, which reappears in the Greek Eos and the Latin Aurora.

785. What is Arusha?

A name for the sun, as he begins his course in the heaven. As such, he is represented as a beautiful child. The name reappears in the Greek Erôs, or god of love, who answers to the

Latin Cupido (Cupid). But Erôs, again, is a son of Iris (another form of the same name), who is called the messenger of the gods; just as Arusha is said to awaken the earth with his rays. These rays become the fiery darts of Eros and Cupid, which inflame with love the hearts that may be pierced by them.

786. Who is Brahma?

He is called a son of Brahm, a name for the Great First Cause of all things. Brahma, Vishnu, and Siva, together make up the later Trimurti or Trinity; Brahma being the creator, Vishnu the preserver, and Siva the destroyer.

787. Is Siva known by any other name?

He is frequently called Mahadeva, or Mahadeo (in Greek, Megas Theos), the *great god*, and is regarded as a reproducer,—to destroy, according to Indian philosophy, being only to reproduce under another form.

788. What are the Avatars of Vishnu?

Incarnations of the god for the accomplishment of a special purpose. The Avatars are fixed as ten in number; when the tenth takes place, the world will be destroyed, and Brahma will again begin his work as creator.

789. Who is Krishna?

A being produced, according to some legends, from one of the hairs of Vishnu, and in his turn producing Rudra, the destroyer. This god became of much greater importance in the later mythology of the Hindus.

790. What is Savitar?

A name for the sun, as golden-handed, in reference to his rays. When the name was taken literally, the story grew up that the sun, offering up a sacrifice, cut off his hand, which was replaced by a golden one.

791. Who is Manu?

A wise lawgiver, and the son of Brahma. He is the same as the Greek Minos: and the name comes from the same root with the words *mind* and *man;* man being so called as the measurer or thinker.

PERSIAN MYTHOLOGY.

792. For what is Persian mythology chiefly remarkable?

For the moral or spiritual meaning which it engrafts on phrases or legends which had reference originally only to physical or material objects. Thus the battle between Indra and Vritra, which in India was a conflict between the god of the sun or heaven, and the dragon which was supposed to shut up the rain, became in Persia the spiritual struggle between moral good and moral evil; and thus a phrase, suggested by a very common sight in the outward world, became the foundation of a philosophy known as Dualism (in other words, the conflict between two gods, one good, the other evil).

793. Were the old names retained in the Persian myths?

In many instances they were. Thus Trita, or Traitana, becomes the Persian Thraetona; while Verethragna, or the *slayer of Verethra*, the Feridún of later epic poetry, answers to the Vedic Vritrahan, or *slayer of Vritra*. Feridún again is the slayer of Zohak (a name which was at first written Azi-dahâka, the biting serpent), or Ahi, which again carries us to the Greek

Echidna. The name Zohak reappears in that of Astyages (Asdahag), the Median king, who is defeated and dethroned by his grandson, Cyrus, as Laios, king of Thebes, is killed by his son Œdipus.

794. Is the germ of this moral idea furnished in the Vedic hymns?

Yes; in the prayer which the worshippers sometimes offer up, that Vritra, the enemy, may not be suffered to reign over them.

795. Was this battle between good and evil denoted by any other names?

It was also spoken of as the great conflict between Ormuzd and Ahriman.

796. What is Ormuzd?

The name of the good god.

797. Is this a Persian word?

No. Nor can it be explained by the Persian language; but in the Zendavesta, the name is given in the form Ahurô-mazdâo, thus carrying us to the Sanskrit words Asuro medhas, which mean *wise spirit*. Another name of Ormuzd was Spentô-mainyus, or the holy spirit.

798. What is the name given in these books to the power which opposes Ahuro-mazdâo?

He is called simply Drukhs, a word meaning *deceit*.

799. What then is the name Ahriman?

It is a name which signifies an evil spirit, and was given at a later time to the power which had been known as Vritra and Drukhs. In the Zendavesta, the holy spirit (Spentô-mainyus, *i. e.* Ormuzd), and the evil spirit (Anrô-mainyus, *i. e.* Ahriman), are said to have created the world.

800. Who are the Devs or Divs?

Spirits whose name is akin to the Greek Theos, and the Latin *deus*. The Zoroastrians separated from the worshippers of the Devas, *i. e.* the Vedic deities, and they declared in their confession of faith in the Zendavesta : "I cease to be a Deva worshipper; I profess to be a Zoroastrian worshipper of Ahuramazda, an enemy of the Devas, and a devotee to Ahura." The Persian Aêshma daêva is the Asmodeus, or *unclean spirit*, of the book of Tobit.

ODIN, THOR, AND FRIGA.

NORSE MYTHOLOGY.

801. What are the chief features of Norse Mythology?

The mythical systems of the tribes of Northern Europe are substantially the same as that of the Greeks. They all have their germ in words or phrases which described the sights and sounds of the material world: but in every country the stories which grew out of this germ were modified by the influences of soil and climate. Thus the mythology of Northern Europe assumed, of necessity, a sombre and gloomy character; and the combat of Phœbus with Python, or of Indra with Vritra, became a constant struggle for life and death.

802. In what story is this struggle described?

In the Volsunga Saga, or tale of the Volsung, which was afterward remodelled in the great epic poem called the Nibelungen Lied, or Lay of the Children of the Mist.

803. Who is the hero of this story?

Sigurd, the son of Sigmund, the son of Volsung, a descendant of Odin.

804. What is the story of his birth?

He was born after the death of his father, and became the foster-child of Regin (the smith of the king of Denmark), who urged him on to slay the dragon Fafnir, who lay coiled on the glistening heath.

805. With what weapon was the dragon slain?

With a sword forged by Regin from the broken bits of Gram.

806. What was Gram?

A sword which Odin himself had driven up to the hilt in an oak-tree, to be taken by him who should be strong enough to draw it out. It was drawn out by Sigmund (the father of Sigurd), who with it conquered every enemy, until

Odin, reappearing in disguise, presented a spear against which it snapped in twain.

807. What followed the death of Fafnir?

Sigurd became possessed of the treasure which lay within his mighty folds, and by eating his heart he also gained a wisdom beyond that of mortal men. Going on his way, he came to a heath, in the midst of which a fierce flame surrounded a house in which the fair maiden, Brynhild, lay asleep. Sigurd rode through the fire, and at his touch she awoke. They then plighted their troth to each other, and Sigurd rode on to the house of Giuki, the Niflung, who determined that he should marry his daughter Gudrun, and that Brynhild should become the wife of his son Gunnar. But Gunnar cannot ride through the flame, and by magic arts Sigurd is made to assume the form and voice of Gunnar, and to hand over Brynhild to him. Discovering his treachery, Brynhild urges Gunnar to slay Sigurd; but, as in the case of Baldr, he and his brothers had sworn not to lay hands on the hero. They therefore got Guttorm to do that which they could not do themselves, and thus Sigurd is slain during his sleep. His death reawakens all the love of Brynhild, who dies heartbroken on his funeral pile.

808. What Greek heroes does Sigurd resemble?

In some or all of his characteristics, he is the counterpart of Perseus, Achilles, Theseus, Phœbus, Phaethon, and Odysseus.

809. To what incident does the driving of the sword Gram into the oak answer?

To the hiding away of the sword and sandals which Ægeus places under a great stone, and of which Theseus gets possession when he is able to lift the stone, and to the weapons which Heracles leaves with Echidna.

810. What is the sword Gram?

It is the same as the invincible spear of Phœbus, and answers also to the armor forged for Achilles by Hephæstus.

811. Who gives this sword Gram to Sigurd?

His mother Hjordis, just as Thetis brings to her son Achilles the armor forged by Hephæstus.

812. What is the slaughter of Fafnir?

It is the same incident as the slaying of Python, Vritra, the Sphinx, Minotaur, and Chimæra.

813. To what does the wisdom of Sigurd correspond?

To that of Iamos and Melampus, both of whom, also, receive it from serpents.

814. Why?

Because the word "dragon" meant simply a far-seeing or keen-sighted being.

815. What is the sleep of Brynhild?

It answers to the slumber of Adonis and Osiris, and to the inaction of the Korê (or maiden) Persephone, in the house of Hades.

816. How is Brynhild won?

After the slaughter of the dragon, just as, after slaying the Libyan monster, Perseus wins Andromeda, and the death of the Sphinx leads to the marriage of Œdipus with Iocastê.

817. What put Brynhild into her deep sleep?

She was wounded with a thorn by Odin, like Isfendiyar in the Persian epic. This thorn of night or of winter answers to the snake-bite which kills Eurydikê in the story of Orpheus.

818. What is the desertion of Brynhild?

It is only another form of the desertion of Ariadne by Theseus, or of Œnone by Paris; and it also answers to the separation of Odysseus from Penelopê, when he leaves her to go to Troy. The return of Sigurd to Brynhild, in the form of Gunnar, answers closely to the return of the disguised Kephalos to Procris, whom he had forsaken.

819. In what relation does Gudrun stand to Brynhild?

In that of Deianeira to Iolê, and of Helen to Œnônê. The desertion is in each case followed by vengeance. Sigurd dies, like Paris, in atonement for his sin. In each case, again, the death of the hero revives the love of the forsaken wife, and Œnone and Brynhild die, each on the funeral pile of her husband.

820. What do we especially notice when we compare this story with other Teutonic legends?

That the poets seemingly could not escape from the charmed circle in which they reproduced, under the disguise of different names, places, and incidents, the great and touching "Tragedy of Nature."

821. Is this seen in the mythical history of the descendants of Sigurd?

Yes. The story is told over again in the case of his son, who is called Ragnar Lodbrog. Like Sigurd, Ragnar wins his first wife Thora by delivering her from a dragon; and, like Sigurd, he forsakes her.

822. What became of Gudrun in the Volsung tale?

She married Atli, the brother of Brynhild; but when Atli slew Gunnar and his brothers, Gudrun in revenge slew her children, and then killed their father Atli himself.

823. Do these incidents answer to any in Greek myths?

The slaying of Atli's children is repeated in the slaughter of the children of Jason by Medea.

824. Who are the Niflungs or Nibelungs?

They are the dwellers in Niflheim, the land or home of the cold mists; in other words, they answer to Phrixus and Helle, the children of Nephele (the mist), who depart with the treasure of the golden fleece just as the Niflungs take away the treasures of the summer.

825. Who was Odin?

A deity who answered to the Greek Zeus, and who is called the Alfadir, or Father of All. His wife is called Freya, or Friga, and she is the mother of Thor and Baldr. The names of Odin and Freya remain in our *Wednesday* and *Friday*, and that of Thor in *Thursday*.

826. How is Thor represented?

With a mighty hammer, as Thor Miölnir, the pounder, thus answering to the Greek Aloadæ and the Indian Maruts.

827. What is the legend of Baldr?

He was the most beautiful of all the dwellers in Valhalla, but although all the other gods had sworn not to hurt him, no oath had been taken from Loki, who destroyed him with the mistletoe. This event answers to the slaying of Isfendiyar with the thorn, and of Adonis with the boar's tusk.

828. What is Loki?

A malevolent deity, described as the great serpent who encircles the earth, and as the father of Hela, the queen of the regions below the earth.

829. What is Valhalla?

The home of Odin, where, like Zeus in Olympus, he dwells with all the Æsir, or gods. Thither are brought the souls of all heroes dying on the battle-field.

830. Who are their guides?

The beautiful Valkyries, or corse-choosers, in whom we see, in a higher and purer form, the Houris of the Mahometan paradise.

831. What are the Norns?

Three sisters who answer to the Fates or Mœræ of the Greeks. Their names are Urd, Werdand, and Skuld (or *Past, Present,* and *Future*). They are represented as beings endowed with a sombre but touching beauty.

832. What is the Twilight of the gods?

This phrase was used to denote the time

when, as it was supposed, the reign of Odin and the Æsir would come to an end.

833. *How could such a notion spring up if Odin was regarded as the Great Maker of all things?*

Because the name Odin was used, perhaps, unconsciously, in more than one sense. Thus Æschylus speaks of Zeus as the Infinite and Eternal God, whose kingdom can never have an end; but when he comes to speak of the mythical Zeus, the son of Cronos and husband of Hera, he says that as Zeus dethroned his father, so would he be himself deposed by a descendant of his friend Prometheus, whom he had so grievously wronged. This overthrow of Zeus by Heracles answers exactly to the Norse Twilight of the gods.

MYTHICAL GENEALOGIES.

The following samples of mythical genealogies, or rather of portions of such genealogies, are given chiefly to show the freedom with which the several Greek States or cities treated their common store of legendary tales. It will be seen at a glance that the several lists present the same names in quite different connections, but that, while it is impossible to reduce them to an historical harmony, they agree strictly with the mythical phrases which furnished the germ of these genealogies, in which gods, heroes, and men are inextricably mingled together.

284   MANUAL OF MYTHOLOGY.

(1) Mythical Genealogy of Argos.

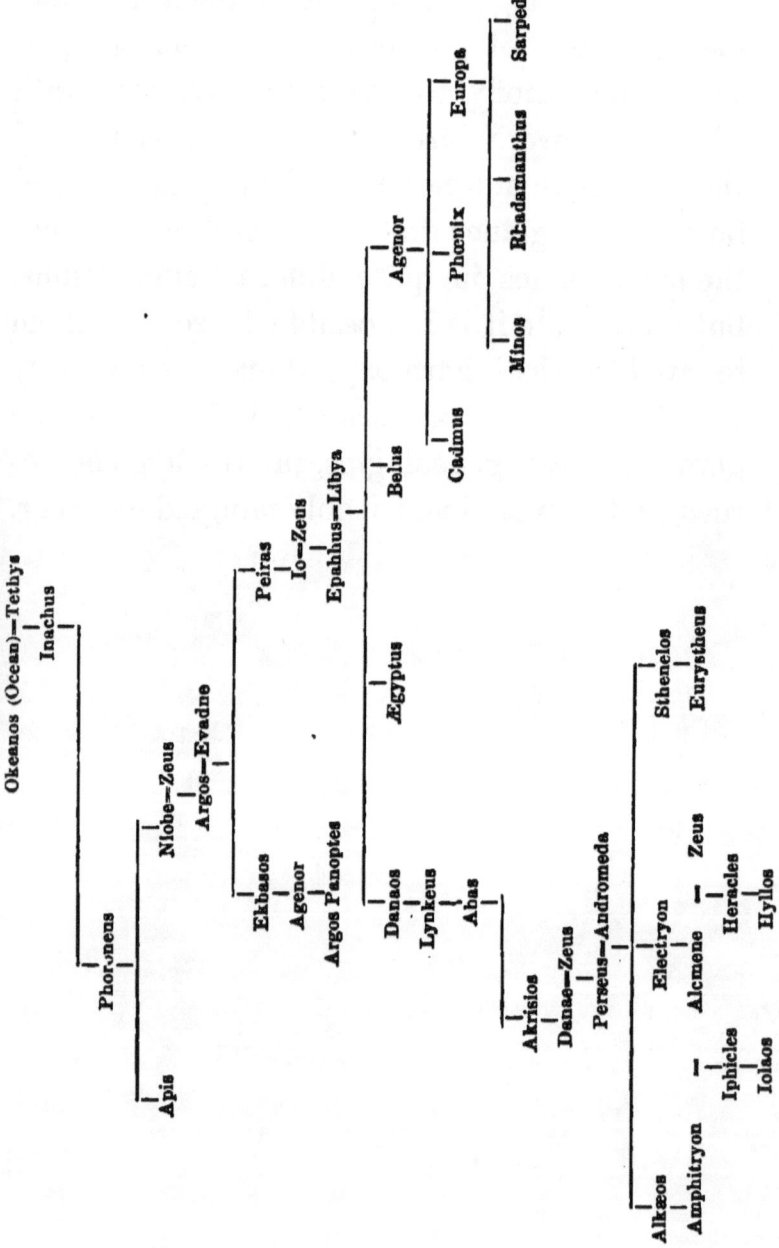

(2) GENEALOGY OF THE IAPETIDS.

```
Okeanos = Gaia
         |
      Iapetus
         |
    ┌────┴──────────────────────────┐
   Atlas                    Prometheus = Pandora
                            Deucalion = Pyrrha
                                    |
                            ┌───────┴────────────────┐
                          Aeolus                Amphictyon   Protogeneia = Zeus
                            |                                          Aethlios
                            |                                          Endymion
        ┌───────────────────┼──────────────┐
      Sisyphus          Salmoneus
        |               Tyro = Poseidon
        |                   |
        |           ┌───────┼───────┐
     Glaucos       Aeson   Pelias  Neleus
     Bellerophon   Jason                Nestor
                    |                   Antilochus
              ┌─────┴─────┐
            Medus       Armenus
```

Dorus Xuthus Ion
       Achaeus

286   MANUAL OF MYTHOLOGY.

(3) GENEALOGY OF THE ÆOLIDS.

```
Æolus
├── Athamas = Nephele
│   ├── Phrixus
│   └── Helle
├── Sisyphus
└── Kalyke = Aethlios
    └── Endymion
        └── Ætolus
            ├── Kalydon
            └── Pleuron
                └── Agenor
                    └── Demonike = Ares
                        └── Thestius
                            ├── Leda
                            └── Althea = Œneus
                                └── Meleagros
```

MYTHICAL GENEALOGY OF THE PELOPIDS.

(4) Genealogy of the Pelopids.

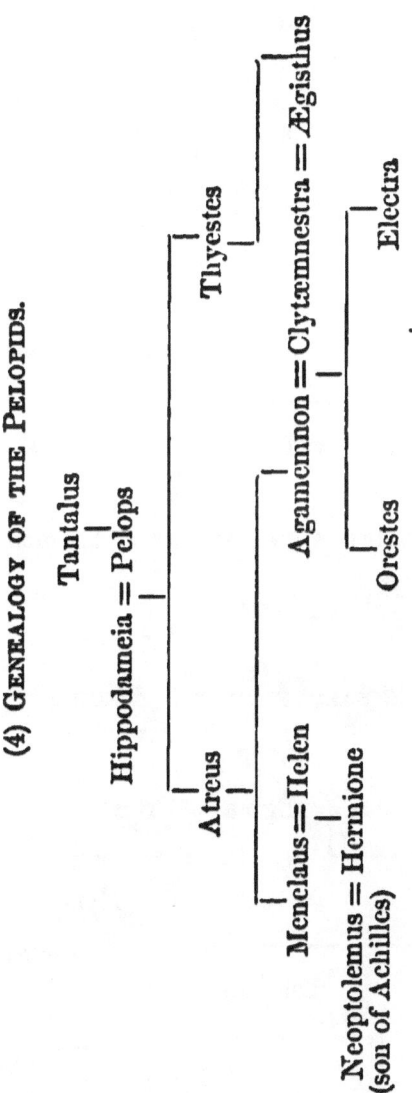

288 MANUAL OF MYTHOLOGY.

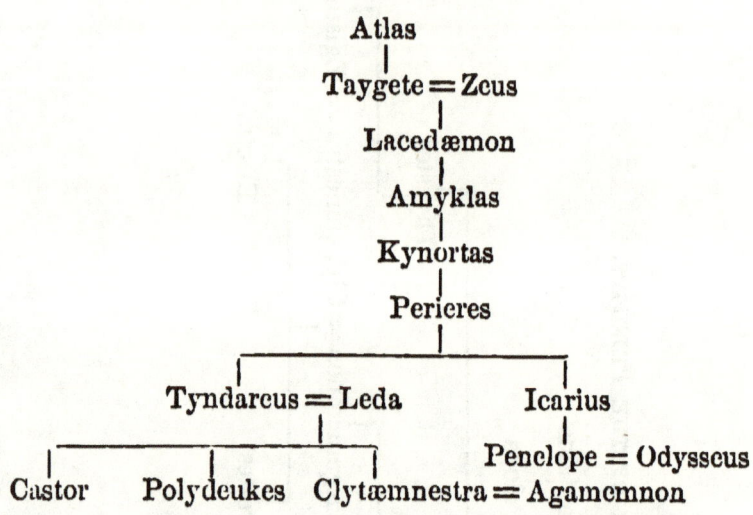

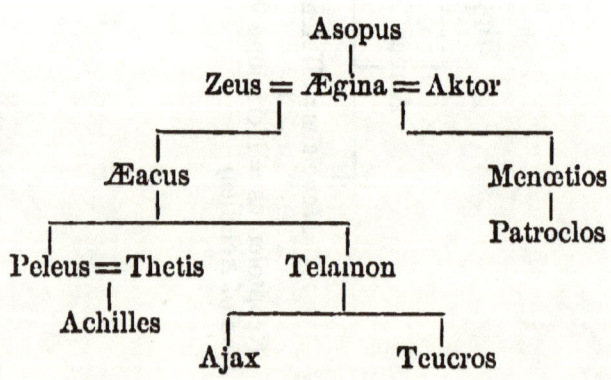

MYTHICAL GENEALOGIES.

(7) Attic Genealogy.

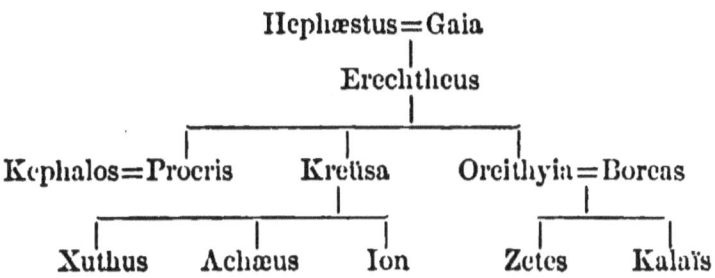

(8) Cretan Genealogy.

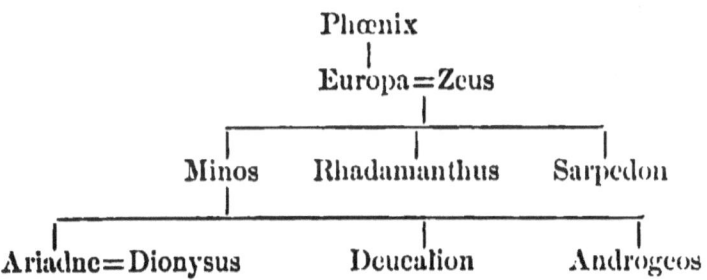

(9) Theban Genealogy.

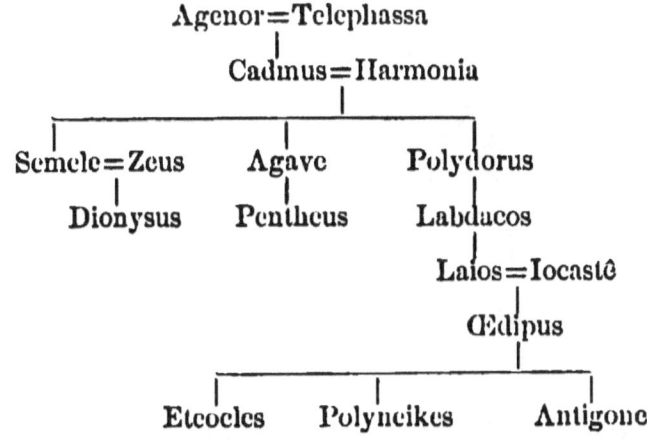

MANUAL OF MYTHOLOGY.

(10) Trojan Genealogy.

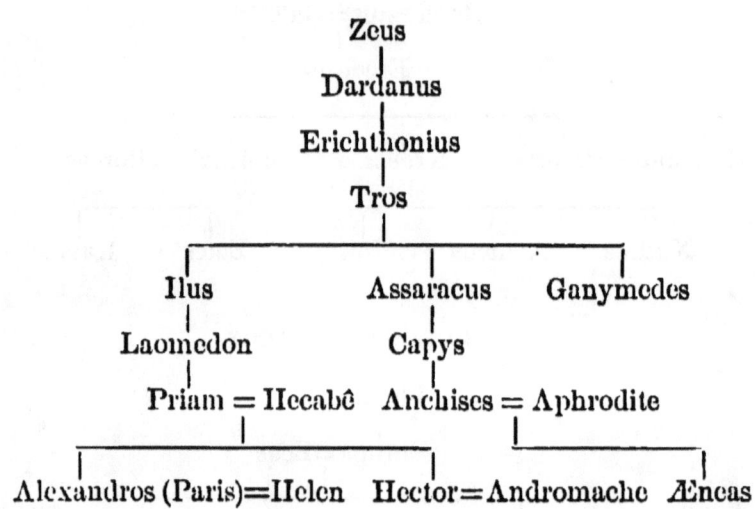

INDEX.

The references are to the Questions.

ACHĔRŌN, 679, 680
Achillĕis, 581
Achillĕs, 14, 23, 41, 61, 577, &c., 597, 605, &c.
Acrĭsĭŏs, 13, 312, 323, &c.
Actōr, 651
Admetus, 60, 206, 300, 443, 448, &c.
Adōnis, 154, 174, &c., &c., 641, 763
Adrammĕlech, 759
Æpȳtus, 519
Æĕtĕs, 539
Ægæ, 59
Ægæon, 528
Ægeus, 342
Ægis, 145, 322, 634
Æglāēr, 443
Ænĕas, 172, 217, 572, 619, 702
Æsculāpius, 206, 440, 709
Aeshma-daēva, 800
Æsir, 829, 832
Æthiōpia, 468, 469
Aĕthlĭos, 463
Æthra, 342, 647, 660
Agamemnon, 162, 579, &c.
Agăvĕ, 260, 410
Agēnōr, 406
Ages, the Five, 485
Aglāīa, 182
Agni, 183, 184, 772
Ahănā, 129, 205
Aharyu, 603
Ahi, 776

Ahrĭman, 795, &c., 799
Ahuromazdāo, 797
Aĭdĕs, 72
Aĭdōnēus, 72
Aisa, 728
Ajax, 567
Akersĕkŏmĕs, 518
Akrĭa, 132
Akshăna, 507, 508
Alcestis, 448
Alcinoüs, 632
Alcmæon, 526
Alcmēna, 262, 305
Alēĭan plain, 513, 514
Alexandros, 561
Alfadir, 825
Alkēstis, 448, &c.
Alkinoüs, 632
Allecto, 386
Alōădæ, 650, 826
Alphēius, 222, 530
Althæa, 414, &c.
Amaltheia, 251.
Amāzons, 468, 472, &c., 53
Ambrōsĭa, 184, 492
Amen-ra, 746
Ammōn, 251, 746
Amphĭărāos, 523
Amphĭōn, 489
Amphĭtrĭtē, 67, 68, 780
Amūlĭus, 13
Anadyŏmĕnĕ, 157
Anammĕlech, 759
Anchīsĕs, 172
Androgĕos, 516

Andromĕda, 320, 335
Andvari, 76
Anankē, 370
Anna Perenna, 739
Aṅrô-mainyus, 799
Anteia, 511
Antigŏnē, 364, 390
Anŭbis, 747
Aornos, 721
Aphrŏdītē, 89, 154, 157, &c.,
566, &c., 663
— Enalia, 167
— Ourania and Pandemos,
167
— Pontia, 167
Apis, 470, 750
Apollo, 14, 46, 138, 186, &c.,
705
Apsyrtus, 542
Arbhu or Ribhu, 400
Arcadia, 48, 426, 444
Arcas, 455
Arctos, 455
Arctūrus, 456
Areiŏpăgus, 155
Arēs, 46, 147, &c.
Arētē, 278
Arētē, 632
Arĕthūsa, 529, &c.
Argeiphontes, 471
Argo, 540, 550
Argonauts, 416, 537, &c.
Argos, 273, 574
Argos Panoptes, 465, &c.
Argos, the dog, 642
Argynnis, 8, 161, 162, 767
Ariădnē, 16, 352, 353
Arjūnī, 161, 767
Artĕmis, 46, 215, &c.,
569
Arusha, 785
Ascălăphos, 567
Ashtaroth, 762
Asklēpĭos, 206, 440, &c., 449,
492, 556

Asmōdeus, 800
Astarte, 762
Astræus, 652
Astyăges, 13
Asuro-mêdhas, 797
Atălanta, 418
Atē, 364, 372, 570
Athēna, 46, 63, 89, 127, &c.,
317, 318, 483
Athens, 144
Athămas, 539
Atlas, 319, 647, 660
Atli, 822
Atrŏpŏs, 371
Augē, 11
Aurōra, 718
Autochthon, 681
Autŏlўcus, 640
Avătār, 788
Avernus, 720
Azi-dahāka, 793

BAAL, or Bel, 755
Bacchus, 710
Baldr, 807, 825, 827
Balios, 64, 438
Beauty and the Beast, 664
Bellerŏphōn, 23, 199, 471,
509, &c.
Bellĕros, 471
Bellōna, 732
Bhuránўu, 8, 236, 783
Bona Dea, 733
Borĕas, 652
Bospŏrus, 468
Brahm, 786
Brahma, 786
Briarĕōs, 528
Briăreus, 528
Brisaya, 412, 603, 767
Brīsēis, 19, 412, 579, 613, 767
Brontē, 30
Brynhild, 16, 206, 287, 335,
336, 500, 807, &c.

INDEX.

CABEIRA, 668
  Cabeiri, 668
Cacus, 711, &c.
Cadmus, 11, 406, &c.
Cæculus, 715
Cæcias, the wind, 715
Calchas, 568, 571
Calliŏpē, 398, 656
Callisto, 455
Calos, 486
Calydonian boar-hunt, 417
Calypso, 631
Camēnæ, 734
Capta, 132
Casandra, 562
Castor, 667
Cattle of Helios, 431, 631
Cĕcrops, 681
Centaur, 19, 275, 498
Cĕphălus, 16, 394
Cerbĕrus, 78, 399, 714
Ceres, 694, 713
Chaos, 28
Chăris, 182
Charītes, 19, 164, 434
Chărōn, 678
Charybdis, 631
Cheirōn, 274, 441
Chemosh, 760
Chīmæra, 14
Chrysāōr, 198
Chrysēis, 579
Cicōnes, 627
Circē, 630
Cleio, 656
Cleopatra, 428, 429
Clōthō, 371
Clymĕnē, 428
Clytæmnēstra, 570
Cōcȳtus, 679, 680
Consentes, 731
Consus, 740
Corōnīs, 206, 440, &c.
Corybantes, 669
Creon, 354

Cretan Labyrinth, 351, 486, &c.
Cretheus, 533
Crisa, 203
Crommyonian sow, 346
Crŏnŏs, 25, 28, 30, 31, 33, 39, 716
Cumæan Sibyl, 720
Cūrētes, 419
Cybĕlē, 670
Cyclopēs, 30, 38, 40, 72, 627, 649
Cyrus, 13, 443, 793

DACTYLI, 669
  Dædălus, 486, &c.
Dagon, 765
Dahănâ, 129, 205, 368, 767
Danăē, 76, 312
Danăi, 717
Daphnē, 18, 204, 767
Dasyu, 374
Daunii, 717
Dēiăneira, 286, 288, 819
Deimos, 171
Delos, 10, 37, 126, 191, 192, 412
Delphi, 196, 202
Dēmētēr, 46, 103, &c., 251
Dēmophŏŏn, 112, 113
Deucălīōn, 39, 458, &c., 544
Devs, or Divs, 800
Dia, 494, &c.
Diāna, 92, 706
Diānus, 92
Dictē, 33, 37, 251
Dictys, 312
Dido, 739
Dii Consentes, 731
Dii Indigĕtes, 730
Diomēdes, 567
Diŏnȳsus, 250, &c., 353, 665
Diŏnē, 158, 251
Dioscūri, 667

Dis, 692
Dōdōna, 48
Dolĭos, 634, &c., 642
Dragon, 557, 813, 844
Drukhs, 798
Dualism, 792
Dyāŭs, 34, 42, 160, 377, 508, 692
Dyāŭspĭtar, 35

ECHO, 535
  Echĭdna, 14, 19, 201, 301, 302, 776, 793
Egeria, 735
Electra, 655
Eleusinian mysteries, 118
Eleusis, 110, 115, 126
Elysĭum, 410
Endymĭōn, 9, 10, 190, 463
Enĭpeus, 532
Enosĭchthon, 57
Enyalĭos, 654
Enyo, 654
Enna, 75, 126
Eōs, 394, 575, 652, 767
Epăphus, 468
Ephĭaltes, 650
Epigŏni, 527
Epimētheus, 480, &c.
Erăto, 656
Erĕbus, 653
Erechtheus, 392, 393
Erĭnȳes, 386
Erinys, 234, 363, 387, 767
Eriphȳle, 525
Eris, 171, 565
Erōs, 171, 178, 661, 664, 785
Erymanthian boar, 283
Eteŏclēs, 364, 525
Ethiopia, 468
Eumæus, 633
Eumenĭdes, 365, 386, 727
Eunŏmus, 288, 289
Eurōpa, 11, 349, 406, &c.

Euryanassa, 493
Eurycleia, 640, &c.
Eurydĭce, 205, 399
Eurydĭke, 205, 399, &c., 817
Eurymĕdōn, 11
Euryphassa, 11
Eurystheus, 14, 266
Eurȳtus, 11, 279, 651
Euterpē, 656
Evadnē, 519, &c.

FAFNIR, 15, 69, 201, 334, 777, 804, 812
Fates, 728
Fauna, 733
Faunus, 733
Favōnius, 659, 742
Feridún, 793
Freya, or Friga, 825
Friday, 825
Frost giants, 649

GAIA, 28, 30
  Gaiēŏchos, 57
Gandharvas, 276, 505
Ganymēdēs, 475
Garānus, 711
Genii, 729
Geryon, 714
Giants, 649
Gigantes, 649
Giuki, 807
Glaŭcus, 572
Glaukē, 354, 544
Glaukōpis, 145
Golden Fleece, 416, 538, 552
Gorgon, 14, 145, 316, 508, 555
Graces, 164, 434, 779
Gradīvus, 741
Graiæ, 302, 317, 318, 332, 333, 654
Gram, 445, 806, &c.

Gudrun, 287, 807, 819, &c.
Gunnar, 807, 822
Guttorm, 807

HADES, 40, 70, &c., 105
  Hæmon, 391
Halirrhŏthĭos, 156
Hamadryads, 646
Harmŏnĭa, 171, 410, 525, &c.
Harits, 59, 165, 434, 779
Har-pi-chruti, 749
Harpies, 283, 655, 673
Harpocrātes, 749
Hĕbĕ, 88, 671
Hecăbĕ, 560, &c.
Hecaergos, 210
Hecăte, 106, 211
Hecătos, 210
Hector, 572, 587, 594
Hecŭba, 560
Helen, 170, 234, 601, 767
Helĭădes, 648
Helĭos, 55, 107, 188, 429, &c.
Hellĕ, 539, 824
Hellĕn, 462
Hellespont, 539, 578
Helli, 578
Hĕmĕrā, 158
Hephæstus, 46, 88, 127, 131, 179, &c.
Hera, 46, 58, 82, &c., 181
Herăcles, 14, 16, 23, 80, 262, &c., 306, 468
Hercŭles, 711, &c.
Hercŭlus, 711
Hermes, 19, 114, 221, &c., 401, 458, 708
Herodŏtus, 475, &c.
Hersĕ, 396, 681
Hesiod, 483
Hesiŏneus, 494, &c.
Hespĕrĭdes, 285, 332
Hespĕrus, 666
Hestĭa, 46, 94, &c.

Hialprek, 185
Hipponoŭs, 509
Hjordis, 811
Homeric Geography, 644
Hōræ, 164
Horus, 749
Houris, 830
Human Sacrifices, 617
Hupnos, 573, 674
Hyădes, 647
Hydra, 283
Hymen, 672
Hyperborean Gardens, 319, 350, 389
Hyperion, 28, 548

IACCHOS, 710
  Ialmĕnos, 567
Iamĭdæ, 519
Iămos, 282, 460, 519, &c., 524, 813, 814
Iapĕtus, 28
Icărus, 486, &c.
Ida, 33, 377, 561
Ilĭa, 700
Iliad, 578, 597, 616
Ilĭon, 558
Inăchus, 465, &c., 489
Indigĕtes, 730
Indra, 15, 19, 349, 367, 368, 557, 602, 622, 774
Ino, 252, 539
Io, 251, 465, &c.
Iobătes, 513
Iocastĕ, 282, 362, &c., 367, 373, 460
Iolcos, 544
Iŏlĕ, 16, 278, 280, 293, 460
Iphĭgĕnēĭa, 217, 218, 568
Iris, 673, 785
Ischys, 441
Isfendiyar, 176, 817
Ishtar, 762
Isis, 470, 748
Ixĭon, 8, 93, 494, &c.

JANUS, 707
Jason, 352, 540, &c., 618, 823
Juno, 90, 688, &c.
Jupĭter, 16, 685, &c., 713
Jupĭter Elĭcius, 687
— Pluvĭus, 687
— Termĭnus, 687
Jŭventas, 671

KAIKĬAS, 715
Kakĭa, 278
Kakĭas, 715
Kebrĕn, 563
Kelĕos, 110, 118
Kephălos, 16, 394, &c., 818
Kēpheus, 322
Kerbĕros, 78, 399
Kikŏnes, 627
Kirke, 630
Kokūtos, 679, 680
Kŏre, 121, 815
Koryphasĭa, 132
Kneph, 746
Krishna, 789
Kÿbele, 670
Kyllene, 222

LABYRINTH of Crete, 352, 486, &c.
Lachĕsis, 371
Ladon, 666
Laertes, 567
Læstrygonians, 630
Laĭos, 13, 326, 358, 374
Lampetĭe, 431, 631
Laŏcŏon,
Laomĕdon, 60, 61, 325
Lares, 722
Larvæ, 725
Laverna, 736
Latĭum, 717
Latmos, 10, 192, 463
Latōna, 10, 705
Leda, 705

Lemŭres, 725
Lernæan Hydra, 283
Lethe, 679, 680
Lēto, 10, 46, 191, 489, &c.
Loki, 827, 828
Lotophăgi, or Lotos-eaters, 627
Lucĕrĭus, 686
Lycia, 126, 192, 412, 454, 574
Lycians, 48, 454
Lucna, 195, 454
Luna, 195, 454
Lycāŏn, 450, &c.
Lykegĕnes, 10, 192, 454

MACUSI Indians, 4
Mahadeo, or Maha-deva, 787
Maia, 221
Mamers, 698
Manes, 724
Manu, 459, 462, 791
Mars, 152, 697, 741, 781
Maruts, 152, 781, 826
Matūta, 695
Mavors, 698
Medēia, or Medĕa, 352, 476, 492, 540, &c., 553, 823
Medūsa, 14, 145, 316, &c., 331, 490
Megæra, 386
Megapenthes, 324
Melampus, 523
Melanthios, 634
Melantho, 642
Meleāger, 199, 414
Meleāgros, 199, 414, &c., 583, 604
Melpomĕne, 656
Memnon, 575
Menelāŭs, 170, 564, &c.
Mercury, 708
Merŏpē, 358
Metaneira, 112, 113

INDEX. 297

Milcom, 759
Minerva, 147, 148, 695
Minos, 462, 517, 791
Minŏtaur, 14, 348
Mœræ, 371, 415
Moira, 371
Moliŏnes, 651
Moloch, 755, 758, &c.
Monēta, 690, 696
Morpheus, 674
Mulcĭber, 741
Muses, 656
Myrmĭdons, 593, 606, &c.

NARCISSUS, 535, &c.
Naubandhăna, 459
Nausicăa, 632
Neāira, 431
Nebo, 761
Nectar, 191, 492
Nĕith, 752
Nelēus, 532
Nemĕsis, 535
Nephĕlē, 539, 824
Neptune (Neptūnus), 691
Nerēus, 55, 188, 429, 691
Nestor, 567
Nessus, 290, &c., 552
Nibelungen Lied, 345, 643, 802
Nibĕlungs, 345, 824
Niflheim, 824
Niflungs, 125, 824
Niŏbē, 489
Nisus, 461, 515, &c.
Norns, 831
Numa, 735
Nysa, 254

OANNES, 765
Odin, 345, 806, 825, 832
Odysseus, 297, 582, 620, &c., 636, 641

Œagros, 398
Œdĭpus, 13, 20, 357, &c.
Œneus, 414
Œnōnē, 16, 206, 563, &c., 599
Ogȳges, 459
Ogygĭa, 631
Olympus, 108
Ops, 716
Oreithyia, 652
Orestes, 570
Orīōn, 657
Ormuzd, 795, &c.
Orpheus, 398, &c.
Orthros, 78, 778
Ortygĭa, 126, 193, &c., 219, 412, 453, 530
Osiris, 748, 815
Otos, 650
Ourănos, 28, 29, 30, 771
Outis, 629

PAIĒŌN, 440
Pallas, 138, 658
Pāles, 726
Palĭcĭ, 726
Pan, 659
Pandăreŏs, 491
Pandōra, 142, 483, &c.
Pani, 602, 767
Parcæ, 727
Păris, 13, 18, 19, 89, 170, 560, &c., 599, 602, 604
Parnassus, 202, 458
Parthĕnōn, 146
Pasiphăē, 348, 349
Patroclos, 438, 573, 585, 608, &c.
Pēgăsus, 512
Pelasgus, 450
Pelēus, 64, 171, 565
Pelĭas, 534, &c., 540, 543
Pelops, 491
Penātes, 723
Peneĭus, 204

Penelŏpē, 351, 487, 622, &c., 633, 639
Pentheus, 258
Periphētēs, 346
Perseus, 13, 14, 23, 73, 199, 249, 304, &c.
Persĕphŏnē, 74, 104, 116, 177, 355
Persĕphassa, 74
Phaĕthŏn, 428, 438
Phaethusa, 431, 631
Phæākia, 631, 644
Phīneus, 321
Philoctētēs, 199, 297, 338
Phlegĕthon, 679, 680
Phlegȳas, 440, 449
Phœbus, 10, 14, 16, 37, 55, 186, &c., 518
Phœnix, the bird, 754
Phœnix, 406, 412, 460, 582
Phœnicia, 407, 412, 453, 574, 644
Phorōneus, 8, 236, 485, 489, 783
Phrixus, 538, &c., 824
Phthah, 752
Picus, 738
Picumnus, 739
Pierĭdes, 656
Pĭĕros, 656
Pilumnus, 739
Pirēnē, 512
Pleiădes, 660
Pluto, 692
Pollux, 460, 667
Polȳbus, 358
Polydectes, 14, 76, 312, 315, 322, 325
Polydegmon, 76, 326
Polydeukes, 460, 667
Polymētis, 487
Polymnia, 656
Polyneikēs, 364, 525
Polyphēmus, 884, 492, 628
Pomōna, 738

Pontus, 28, 56
Poseīdōn, 40, 52, &c., 96, 325
Potnĭa, 57
Prætus, 511
Pramantha, 474, 703
Priam, 13, 562, &c., 596
Priāpus, 663
Procris, 16, 217, 392, &c., 405, 818
Procrustes, 346
Prodĭcus, the Sophist, 277
Promēthēūs, 39, 141, 236, 458, 467, &c., 783
Prōteus, 257, 662, 668, 765
Proserpĭna, 692
Protogeneia, 462, &c.
Prytanēium, 99
Psȳchē, 664
Psychŏpompos, 244
Pyriphlegĕthōn, 679, 680
Pyrrha, 458, 460
Python, 14, 69, 200, 201

Q UIRĪNUS, 701

R A, 753
Ragnar Lodbrog, 821
Recarānus, 711, 713
Regin, 185, 345, 804
Remus, 699, &c.
Ribhu, 400
Rishis, the Seven, 457, 459, 782
Romŭlus, 13, 443, 699, &c.
Rudra, 789
Rustem, 15, 176

S ALMŌNEUS, 553
Sărāmā, 231, 233, 574, 601, 767
Sarānȳū, 232, 387, 388, 767

INDEX.

Sarpēdōn, 232, 373, &c., 574
Sarvăra, 79, 714
Saturn, 716
Savītar, 790
Scylla, 462, 515, 631
Seirens, 631
Selēnē, 9
Selli, 578
Semēlē, 251, 252, 253, 261
Semo Sancus, 739
Serāpis, 751
Set, or Seth, 748
Seven Sages, 457
Shamas, 760
Shemesh, 760
Sidēro, 533
Sigurd, 15, 16, 69, 76, 185, 287, 302, 604, 803, &c.
Sigmund, 345, 803, &c.
Silēnus, 677
Silvānus, 738
Sinis, 346
Sintians, 181
Sipўlus, 491
Sisўphus, 510
Siva, 786, &c.
Skuld, 832
Skylla, 462, 515, &c., 631
Solўmi, 513
Spentô-mainyus, 797, 799
Sphinx, 14, 20, 201, 360, &c., 378, &c., 492, 777
Sterŏpē, 30
Stymphālus, 283
Styx, 679, 680
Symplēgădes, 540

TAMANAKS, 464
Tammuz, 174, 763
Tantălus, 20, 289, 491, &c.
Tartărus, 30
Tēlemăchus, 438, 634, &c.
Telĕphassa, 11, 406, &c.
Telĕphus, 11
Telphusa, 200

Termīnus, 687
Terpsīchŏrē, 656
Teutamīdas, 823
Thaleia, 656
Thanătos, 300, 448, 573
Thaumas, 655
Thebes, 409
Thĕmis, 191
Theogonies, 48
Thermōdon, 472
Theseus, 14, 16, 23, 199, 302, 341, &c., 365
Thĕtis, 58, 170.
Thĕtis, 529, 565, 590
Thor, 825
Thor Miölnir, 651, 781, 826
Thora, 821
Thraĕtăna, 69
Thriæ, 230, 246
Thrinakīa, 631
Thucўdīdes, 478
Thursday, 825
Thyōnē, 261
Tiphys, 540
Tiryns, 324
Tisiphone, 386
Titarēsius, 49
Titans, 38
Tithōnos, 576
Tiu, 35
Traitana, 69
Trimurti, 786
Triptŏlĕmus, 113
Trita, 68, 135, 780
Tritopătōr, 68
Tritogeneia, 68, 133, 780
Triton, 68, 133
Trolls, 649
Troy, 558, &c.
Troy, Tale of, 600, &c.
Tuesday, 35
Twilight of the gods, 833
Typhaon, 200
Typhon, 384
Tyro, 532

INDEX.

URANIA, 656
   Uranus, 28, 771
Urd, 831
Ushas, 719, 767, 784

VALHALLA, 829
   Valkyries, 380
Varuna, 29, 770, &c.
Venus, 702, &c.
Vertumnus, 738
Verethra, 793
Verethragna, 793
Vesta, 102, 693
Vishnu, 786, &c.
Volsung, 803
Volsunga Saga, 802
Vritra, 15, 79, 201, 334, 383, 775, &c.
Vritrăhan, 793
Vulcan, 183, 704, 741

WEATHERSKY, 662
   Wednesday, 825

Werdand, 831
Wooden Horse, 676

XANTHOS, the horse, 64, 438, 592
Xanthos, the stream, 574
Xerxes, 202
Xisuthrus, 459, 764

YAMA, 79, 778

ZAGRĔOS, 665
   Zephўrus, 673
Zeus, 24, &c., 40, 41, 46, 58, 77, 129, 482, 771
Zeus-păter, 35
Zeus Ephestĭos, 50
—— Horĭos, 687
—— Horkĭos, 50
—— Xenĭos, 50
Zio, 35
Zohak, 69, 793

www.ingramcontent.com/pod-product-compliance
Lightning Source LLC
Chambersburg PA
CBHW032042230426
43672CB00009B/1437